CONFIDE: THE NEW PSYCHOLOGY OF CONFIDENCE

CONFIDE: THE NEW PSYCHOLOGY OF CONFIDENCE

How to Power Up after Experiencing Depression

ADAM BOWCUTT

To order additional copies of this book, contact:
Xlibris
1-800-455-039
www.Xlibris.com.au
Orders@Xlibris.com.au
783409

This book is dedicated to and in loving memory
of the following beautiful human beings:

Grandad
Colin Dalziel
Christopher Butcher

Rest In Peace

CONTENTS

INTRODUCTION

Why did I write this book?

I almost ended my life. I'm so glad I didn't because my beautiful son, Zachary now has a mentally healthy and confident father to love him, and for him to love.

It could have ended in tragedy. A son without a father? A family without their son? Sister's without their brother? Friends without their friend?

Almost one million humans take their lives each year in this world. That's one beautiful human every forty seconds. This is the reality. This is tragic.

It is preventable.

I will now share with you my story and 'How to Power Up after Experiencing Depression'.

How I went from zero confidence to rock-solid mental health.

'The best way to find yourself is to lose yourself in the service of others'. - Gandhi

It is now my life mission to help *save 500,000 lives from suicide, one life at a time.*

I wrote this book because change starts with us. It starts with you. It starts with me, myself, and I.

Let's *start*, shall we?

"What happened, mate?"

I went through four episodes of serious clinical depression. I was hospitalised—once in my twenties, another time in my mid to late twenties, a third time in my late thirties, and most recently, a couple of years ago.

One year is the time it took for me to regain 'normality'

This time was different.

One year of time—time you don't get back. Time is limited, and time is the most important asset we don't own. Time is massively valuable, so each time, I had to rebuild myself. I had to rebuild my confidence, my health, my mental health, my physical health, my financial health, and my life.

How did I regain balance?

I was disconnected. My son, Zachary, was around two years old at the time.
Looking back, I now realise I was depressed for about two years prior.

The most important event to happen in my life was my son being born on 30 June 2014.
It was indescribable.

I wrote a poem about it, and you can find it in Kimberley Chakona's book, *Poetry to the People*. You'll soon read the excerpt in this book. I've also written the original raw version for you to read. No filters.

After my last bout of serious clinical depression, I was admitted to the psychiatric ward of the local hospital. My mental health and confidence was at an all-time low. Level zero.

I exercised regularly in hospital. Physically, I felt healthy. But, mentally, I was not.

After being discharged from hospital it was only a matter of weeks before I was readmitted. two steps forward and three steps back. It was frustrating and disappointing.

As human beings, we need a balance of physical and mental health. In my opinion, mental health is more important than physical health. Your mental health and mindset affect almost everything in your life. They are connected to your physical health too.
So I want to show you how I rebuilt myself. I had no confidence. You'll learn how I rebuilt my self myself.

I rebuilt my mental health into a rock-solid foundation. I went on a journey to piece together and mould a super-strong and stable base of mental health.

After experiencing depression, I had almost zero confidence. Now to this day, my confidence, mental health, and mindset are as strong as they have ever been, and they are getting stronger every single day.

What you do daily is critical.

What you do every single day, every single morning, creates your reality, your personal reality, your personality, and your life.

I am enthusiastically sharing with you my mission to help save 500,000 lives from suicide, one life at a time. Today, I am 40 years of age, and I am going to live to 100. You just watch me! This means I have 60 years of purposeful work to complete this life mission.

I will never, never, never give up on my mission to save 500,000 lives from suicide.
Victory against suicide will happen one life at a time.

Please continue to read this book. I hope you have fun with it. I hope you enjoy reading it.
I'm certain you'll learn from it.

This book is broken down into three categories for most chapters.

1 CHOOSE

2 AWARENESS

3 NOW

How to use this book:

Each chapter has a *power-up number*, 9 is the strongest

1C + 2A + 3N = ***POWER***

This book will help you, the beautiful humans you love, friends, neighbours, strangers, anyone in the wider community, and any human being power up after experiencing depression. It will help rebuild a rock-solid foundation of super-strong mental health. Once we all have a solid foundation of mental health and mindset, it is highly likely humans won't get to the stage of wanting to or feeling as if they need to end their own lives.

If someone ends their life, they have decided to murder themselves. How bad does it have to be? How bad is your life and how you feel and think about it, to get to the stage where you want to take action and kill yourself?

In my personal experience, I almost killed myself.

My mental health was so weak, so broken; my mind was so ill and filled with sickness and disorder—dirt. My emotions, use of logic, and mental health were not functioning healthily. It was so unhealthy and rotten that I got to the stage where I googled 'how to kill yourself'.

I got some rope. After learning how to tie a noose, I walked steadily down the steps to my garage. I calmly made a noose and tied it to the top of the horizontal bar and frame of the electric garage door. I got a red bucket and turned it upside down for me to stand on.
I placed the noose around my neck and tightened it. I stood on the red bucket, and I was going to do it. At this point, I was not thinking about anyone else. It was just me, pure ego—me, myself, and I. I thought, *How can this problem be solved? How can I end this constant suffering, and how can I end my life?* It was almost an obsession, a fascination, a fixation.
Right, I'm doing it. I am almost there.
I tightened the noose to the extent where it almost couldn't be made loose again.

This is a poem I wrote that attempts to explain my experience of despair. Progressing to mental repair.

————————

To Die Today?

————————

My frown reflects like deep emptiness mocking me from another dimension.

Stained sparingly with splatters of escaped toothpaste, the bathroom mirror reveals a broken spirit.

Who is that sorry excuse of a man staring back from the stained glass?

"You useless piece of shit" a voice declared with venom.

"Kill yourself" the voice said hissing like an angry snake.

This will be another long night.

Now, awake from disjointed slumber. What's today? Just another number.

Days meaningless and nights drawn-out.

What's the point of life poisoned with doubt?

Fear hits my body like a bolt of lightning.

To die today?

Shallow breath and pounding heart. Will I ever see the light?

With noose held tight I walk downstairs.

I've lost the fight. I'm in despair.

Now in the garage. Around my neck, I tighten the rope. Is it over yet?

There is no hope.

Stood upon the red bucket turned on its head. Ready to drop I just can't cope.

"If you fail what then?"

A broken mind and shattered body? A human shell with a stale soul?

Good night, lights out.

Tomorrow comes, so what now?

"Do you want to join me on a journey?" An Angel pleads.

What's the worst that can happen I mused because yesterday was severe.

"Yes" I gently replied. The Angel nodded knowingly.

We drove to Sydney on a chariot searching for hope.

An environment of new state freshened my mind.

Time well spent with loved ones truly nourishing.
Mind quenched by life's water at source.

Now, it's time to flow and let the past go.

Peace
———

———

———

I have a question for you.

Are you okay?

Are you really okay?

The problem is, men usually don't ask for help when they're not okay, and this is very dangerous. Why is asking for help important? Specifically a man asking for help when they're not okay.

Number one, it saves lives. You can save a life, be it your life or the life of another human being.

———

Number two, it helps build confidence.

Number three, you realise that leadership is a choice.

A powerful foundation of confidence can be created by building valuable leadership skills with a focus on leadership without title.

A few years ago, I was in a relationship that started to go downhill. We lost connection with each other. My work life was struggling, and I was experiencing lots of stress, without much passion in my work. I wasn't sleeping or eating well. My mind was rushing and constantly all over the place.

I was a new father. The scale of this responsibility affected my mind too. I started to become depressed and anxious, and I got to the stage where I wasn't sleeping.
Without sleep, my brain was fading. My mind wasn't working correctly, and then it got to the stage where I was hospitalised because I was a danger to myself.

This was the lowest point in my life. I got a red bucket and turned it upside down and stood on it.

I wrapped the noose around my neck. At this moment, was I about to end my life?

In my broken mind it was like a slow-motion video. I felt no hope throughout my entire being. I felt hopeless, with no thought for the future. I thought, *If I do this now and it doesn't work, I'm going to be paralysed. Therefore, I won't be able to complete my goal of ending my own life.* So I didn't do it. In that moment, logic saved me.

I was still very depressed and anxious. How was I going to build myself back up from there?

Thankfully, my sister Natalie, this altruistic angel, was there with me. Three days after I was discharged from the psychiatric ward, she said,'

Please, please, please, will you come on a journey with me?'

'I'm listening,' I said, in anticipation of what was to be.

She began to explain the plan: hire a Winnebago and drive from Brisbane to Sydney to spend time healing in a new environment. My mother, Rosita, who was flying from England to Australia to be with me, would be with us too.

I had nothing to lose—well, except my life!

—

So I said, '*Yes!* Let's do this, shall we?'

Spending quality time with family, relaxing, playing board games, eating healthily, and walking and spending time in nature—it was extremely nourishing for my mind and body.

What's the solution, and how did I rebuild myself back up to this present day?

Number one: Move your body—move obviously, voluntarily, energetically.

Start small.

For example:

- one-minute walk
- five star jumps
- ten-minute swim
- thirty-second run.

Whatever you do, please move your body; moving your body and changing your physiology can have awesome effects on your mind and mindset, because it builds momentum. It builds energy to get your body moving by tricking your brain into thinking 'I'm energised because I'm moving'. So your body instructs your brain, in addition to your brain instructing your body. It's powerful and self-reinforcing in that once you start, it's relatively easy to maintain.

I started off with yoga. It was helpful in getting my body moving to create momentum, because it was gentle.

Build a network of support. It could be family, friends, colleagues, or neighbours. Choose people you can talk to about anything at any time. If you don't know anyone you can talk to about anything at any time, then the time to change this is now. Right now!

Make a list. Whose presence do you feel comfortable in? Pick the person you know deep down would listen to you and help.

Did you know that human beings need connection? You can, in fact, die from loneliness.

So what are you waiting for? Reach out and build your network. Do it now.
Right now.

- Send a quick message - text, messenger, email etc

- Call a friend

- Connect with three people by asking them this question: will you please help me if I'm ever in need of moral support?

This is my personal favourite, and it is massively powerful: meditate regularly. Meditating, for me, is like going to the gym for my mind. The mind gym. In order to build up strength and resilience with mental clarity, you must do it regularly.

If we go to the mind gym once a month, we won't get great results, whereas if we go every day we will build mental strength.

You can download an app. I like One Giant Mind. There are many others to choose from too.

What is meditation?

It's the personal practice of being 'in the moment', without distractions from the past or future—being present.

By simply focusing on your breathing, you can meditate in the shower. Whatever works for you.

Start with thirty seconds, and build gradually to five minutes, then ten minutes. I meditate for nine minutes every day, and it is one of the most important parts of my daily practices. It's the best thing I've ever committed to, because it builds mental clarity. It gets you in the present moment and grows mental strength, creativity, and most importantly, happiness.

Now how can you feel better?

It feels absolutely amazing to help others; you can feel good by making other people feel good, and there are so many benefits to helping others.

'The best way to find yourself is to lose yourself in the service of others.' This is my favourite quote of all time.

Look at yourself in the mirror. You can say this out loud or say it in your mind. Ask yourself this important question:

Are you okay?

Truly think about the question deep in your entire being. Your soul, so to speak. Then feel your answer come to you with honesty.

Remember to ask for help. This is critical and could literally save countless lives. Pick one person you trust, and genuinely ask for help by simply saying these five empowering words:'

Please, will you help me?'

Do it.

Then ask three other people. Asking for help is a sign of incredible strength and is definitely not a sign of weakness.

It's my mission to change the mindset around this issue and to lead by example by being vulnerable.

You are awesome.

You deserve to have an awesome life.

I am grateful for your valuable time.

Thank you.

Now, in your own time, please continue to read and absorb the words in this book.

These words could save a life.

1

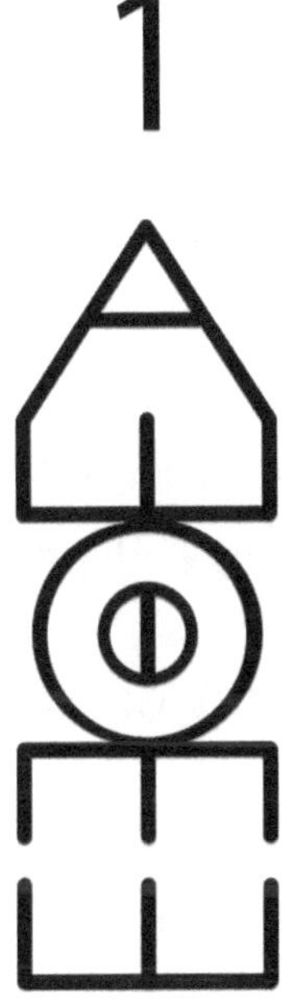

CHOOSE LEADERSHIP

Power-up score: 9

The best way to find yourself is to lose
yourself in the service of others.
Gandhi

When I say the word *leadership*, what images, words,
thoughts, and feelings spring to mind?

Okay, now come with me on a journey into the new psychology of confidence, with massive respect to leadership. You see, leadership is a choice. You can either choose to be a leader or not.

The challenge is that too many people hold on to a belief that they are not a leader or that they can't become a leader. The belief that you have to be chosen to be a leader is a popular one.

The reason it's critical to decide to choose leadership is that it's either a lifetime of waiting or a lifetime of doing great things every single day.

Okay. Are you ready for one of the most important questions of your life?

Will you choose leadership?

Yes or no?

Okay.

What is your answer?

I seriously hope you said yes.

Yes?

Awesome! Great choice.

Now we can get to work and have fun creating your future. Let's do this shall we?

Did you know that leadership is a learnable skill?

Just over a year ago, I felt I was a leader. Quietly, I've always felt this. But I didn't believe it because I held on to a false belief that I had to be given a leadership title. Oh, how wrong I was. That day, I made a clear decision. I chose to be a leader. I committed to leadership, and my life changed instantly.

My energy levels were high, and I possessed a powerful sense of purpose. Why?

The reason was that I took control of life. I accepted responsibility for my actions and knew it was all up to me. It was like my body and mind united to absorb energy, recharge, and be prepared for the long journey ahead. So leadership is definitely a choice. You'll be in a great position to help so many people improve their lives through your actions and behaviour. How does that sound?

> 'If your actions inspire others to dream more,
> learn more, do more and become more,
> you are a leader'. - John Quincy Adams

Will you join me on this epic journey? I guarantee it will be fun, enlightening, and full of knowledge and personal growth. Most importantly, you will learn to powerfully harness your energy in the valuable form of confidence.

'Confidence is the key to almost everything in life'.
The Author

There are countless explanations about what being a leader is. The most important is your perception of leadership, because perception is reality. It's your personality. Personal reality.

1 CHOOSE

As human beings, we are limited by our brain's functions, but we are definitely unlimited in how we utilise our brain. We have consciousness. 'I think, therefore I am,' said a rather thoughtful human named Descartes.

Self-awareness is critical here.

How self-aware are you?

Your DNA determines your leadership style. Self-awareness is most important in leadership. How can you lead others if you can't lead yourself? Truly knowing who you are—your values, strengths, and weaknesses—will help you lead yourself so that you can effectively lead others. So who are you?

Grab a clear sheet of paper and a pen or note down on your phone the following:

I am
I am
I am

Now fill in the empty space that follows 'I am'

How did you go?

If you found this easy – great! If not, welcome to the daily challenge of being a human being.

Revisit the above daily and check in with what you think and write. The sooner you become clear with knowing who you are, the better. Especially with respect to choosing leadership.

How will you strengthen your self-discipline? Keep reading to learn more.

2 AWARENESS

Visualise in your mind's eye a crystal-clear vision of certainty. What does certainty specifically look like to you? For me, I see and feel a guarantee of my future. I am sharing my voice with millions of people to effect change as a leader. I have helped save 500,000 people from suicide, with Victory Against Suicide.

Simple Life Advice

Do you sometimes find it difficult making decisions?

If so, use this effective tool to help you learn how to make effective decisions: Type into Google: "*the Decision-Maker* by Seymour Schulich"

Okay, so now you've decided. What now?

Practise every single day. Practise leadership skills. By consistently helping others reach their goals and become successful, you will, in turn, become a great leader. Remember, the meaning of success is different to everyone.

Okay, great! So you know who you are and lead yourself authentically with self-discipline. You're passionate about helping others. Now what?

To become a great leader, you'll need to learn, practise, and master a mix of important leadership skills.

Confidence. For your followers to have confidence in you, you'll need to radiate confidence. Good job for reading this book then!

Communication. Effective and enthusiastic communication is critical in creating a clear understanding of your vision and purpose.

Relationships. Build and nurture strong long-term relationships, because trust is a foundation of leadership.

There are many other leadership skills to learn. For example, delegation, strategy, and lifelong learning—always be learning.

An exponential principle of leadership is a focus on creating more leaders. It's about succession and legacy. As a masterful leader, you'll help build a better world by creating progressive and adaptable leaders.

In whichever space and time you're in, you will solve problems and have influence, now and in the future. It's exciting!

'Lead, so when you leave, your influence remains'.
The Author

It's not easy being a leader. Nothing worth doing ever is.

3 NOW

Now go practise.

* * *

My friend, and fellow optimist, Victor Perton asked me some great questions for The Australian Leadership Project.

Victor Perton: Adam, what is your favourite story of a contemporary Australian leader?

Adam Bowcutt: Janine Allis, founder of Boost Juice. She's a naturally warm leader of service, with high standards. Janine started from humble beginnings on a kitchen table into multiple franchises worldwide. She's inspirational. She won the Innovation Initiative Of The Year Award 2017.

Victor Perton: Adam, what are the unique qualities of Australian Leadership and leaders?

Adam Bowcutt: They are grounded and practical with great vision to help create a better Australian future for all.

Victor Perton: Adam, what do Australians want of their leaders?

Adam Bowcutt: Honesty and integrity.

Victor Perton: Adam, who have been the leaders in your life's journey?

Adam Bowcutt: Marc Frank Montoya, Mariana Martinelli and my mother, Rosita Bowcutt

Victor Perton: Adam, who or what has inspired you?

My unique spirit—my DNA—Adam Bowcutt. Arnold Schwarzenegger, Richard Branson, Elon Musk and Gary Vaynerchuk.

* * *

"I am a leader".

* * *

Now, it's your turn.

"I am a leader"

Say "I am a leader" out loud three times.

It's a great start.

2

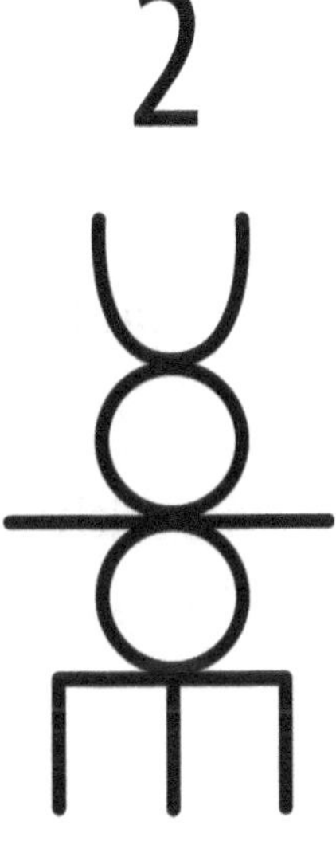

BUILD CONNECTIONS

Power-up score: 8

You are the average of the five people
you spend most of your time with.

People won't remember what you said, but they
will always remember how you made them feel.

The word *listen* contains the same
letters as the word *silent.*

1 CHOOSE

Build your connections.

- Important because: human relationships make up the fabric of your life, along with everyone else connected to you in some way, now and in the future.

- Important because: without relationships, you could die of loneliness—literally.

Did you know you can die from loneliness? A study concluded, 'Actual and perceived social isolation are both associated with increased risk for early mortality.' 'Loneliness—both its objective state and feelings of loneliness—is also the psychological state most associated with suicide, to the point where it's safe to say that while not all lonely people are suicidal, all suicidal people are lonely' (https://www.forbes.com/sites/quora/2017/01/18/loneliness-might-be-a-bigger-health-risk-than-smoking-or-obesity/#59a9506e25d1).

I have a small network of snowboarder friends I'm still in touch with. They are rad! Since moving to Australia, I have proactively built up my network deep and wide. It's amazing.

- Join a community of like-minded people and offer to contribute and help.

- Ask for help.

You will build confidence by building your network. It's a mutually reinforcing cycle; this means you will become more confident as your network grows, and as your network grows, you will, in turn, become yet more confident. It's exponential, where one plus one doesn't equal two, but one plus one equals three. Two minds connecting and collaborating create more than the sum of their parts.

2 AWARENESS

- Important because: psychologically, humans are social creatures. Without a society to belong to, it's all too easy to become isolated from the group and become a lone wolf. What do you think ultimately happens to a lone wolf?

- Important because: by building connections, you are creating and maintaining a valuable support system. If you need to reach out, there are friends, colleagues, business associates, and family to help you in times of need. Mentally and psychologically, this is a great boost of confidence, because you know people have your back. Likewise, I'm sure you'd have theirs too.

Did you know that the deeper and larger a person's network, the higher their net worth?

At university, I entered the university halls alone, shy and nervous. I plucked up the courage to introduce myself to my roommates. 'Hello, my name's Adam. Can I come to dinner with you, please?' It was later revealed that they thought I was a random stranger. Fast-forward ten plus years and we are the best of friends to this day. We have a WhatsApp group chat, all seven of us. It's a melting pot of British banter. It's like we are still at university!

- Take a deep breath. Visualise what will happen in your mind. If you're feeling nervous, reframe it as excitement. Imagine that this stranger is an old friend and that you're greeting him for the first time in three years. Think 'What is the worst that can happen?' and then do it! It gets easier, I promise. 'Strangers are friends you haven't met yet.'

- When you meet someone new for the first time, check their eye colour, because that moment of focus will create a great first impression; you'll connect on a deeper level purely by using great eye contact and body language. The halo effect will come into play. For example, they will think 'Wow, this person is confident and is really focused on me and wants to connect'. Try it. Seriously, it works!

Once you start to truly connect with others in the moment, you will begin to build valuable connections that will help you now, one year from now, or ten years from now. It doesn't matter when. The most important thing is to start. Do it. Now.

3 NOW

When you truly, authentically, and deeply connect with people, a foundation of trust is built.

- Important because: a lifetime of solid friendships and strategic partnerships, in life and business, is the outcome. Friendships are built on trust. 'Help me, Obi-Wan Kenobi.

You're my only hope' (Leia Organa). You need friends to get you out of tight situations and vice versa.

- Important because: you will be a force to reckon with alongside your powerful alliances. People do business with people they trust. Your network = strength in numbers.

Did you know you can practise relational mastery? It's powerful because it helps you draw from ancient knowledge and wisdom, with respect to your human interactions in daily life.

I used to think the friends you grow up with are the most important people you build connections with. I found out this is not the case, because once you become an adult—and even before that, in some cases—you can choose your friends.

- Show up to events you're invited to, or even better, go to events you pick that you're interested in. For example, if you like fishing, go to a fishing event or meetup. You'll be glad you did, because the benefit of meeting like-minded people will lift your spirits. Use the force. Try it. Go on!

- Once you're over your initial fear of meeting a stranger for the first time, reveal something honest and true about yourself in pleasant conversation. For example, I love the peace and quiet of sitting at the local river because it's relaxing. Or if you're feeling a bit more daring, perhaps share that you once kissed a fish and felt more connected with it than with your partner! See what happens. If you're vulnerable with other people, their defence forces will begin to lower. This will build trust. Trust is ultimately what connections and deep friendships are based on. Do it.

You have the power to choose each day who you will connect with. Start today! Who will you connect with and why?

Do it. Now. Send a quick message via email, messenger, instagram etc "Hey, I am ….. and I like how you …."

Building connections is massively important to your quality of life, especially your bank balance, because it is said that 'your network is your net worth'. What does this mean? Well, it means the value of your connections is inextricably linked to who you know.

- Important because: you've heard the phrase 'It's not what you know, it's who you know', yes? There's certainly a grain of truth there. Let's not disregard the hunger for knowledge, because your authentic connections with people in your network afford you valuable knowledge, in context. It is not just book smarts. It's great to read and absorb knowledge. Gaining knowledge from others, in context, offers a rich source of knowledge, leading to wisdom. Knowledge is knowing information. Wisdom is the ability to use relevant knowledge effectively to improve your life and the lives of others.

- Important because: a support network is invaluable to your mental health if you're feeling low or had a crappy day, or if symptoms of stress, anxiety, or depression begin to rear their ugly head. With a strong and deep network of people that know your background, they'll be there for you, to help you through challenging times. Likewise, I'm sure you'd do the same for them. Wouldn't you?

Did you know networking is one of the most important skills in business?

As my mental health started to strengthen, I knew of the importance of networking. I got out of my comfort zone and went to a networking event. I felt so awkward. *What should I do? How should I introduce myself?* I thought. An array of limiting beliefs started to flood my mind. *What will they think of me? Am I good enough? What if I make a fool of myself?* I used my own mantra of 'What is the worst that can happen?' Just as I was about to pluck up the courage to say 'Hello, my name's Adam. What's yours?' a friendly gentleman in a smart suit beat me to it! He took the words right out of my mouth, except he said his name first. It was absolutely fine. What on earth had I been worrying about? We had a pleasant chat. What I noticed was how much he focused on how he could help me. It was a welcome change to meeting people who only talked about themselves. I was inspired to get better at networking, do it regularly, offer to help people, and make sure I focused on them. It felt good.

LinkedIn is a great resource too. I met an amazing leader and was invited to do a presentation. I felt the fear and did it anyway. Beyond fear is growth.

- Get out of your comfort zone. Show up! Force yourself to go to an event where there will definitely be other people in the same situation as you. Set a challenge where the goal is to introduce yourself to at least one person in the first fifteen minutes.

- Focus on how you will offer to help the other person. Listen closely to what they're about by asking open questions enthusiastically—what, when, where, how, who, and my favourite, why. You can start online via LinkedIn too.

Building connections is a sure-fire way to build a powerful network that will serve you and, most importantly, help you be of service to others now and in the future. Start networking now!

Three Challenges:

- Approach a colleague at work that you don't know and introduce yourself. Hi my name is... Then ask them how their day is going and really listen.

- Approach a person you don't know that you find attractive and introduce yourself. Hi my name is... Then ask them how their day is going and really listen. (This challenge is limited to those of you that are single)

- Approach a person you are inspired by, it could be a manager, business leader, celebrity. Introduce yourself and ask them how their day is going and really listen.

Pick one and commit to completing the challenge. Make yourself accountable by telling a friend or relative what your challenge is and when you'll do it. This way you're more likely to take action

* * *

'The measure of intelligence is
the ability to change.
Einstein

3

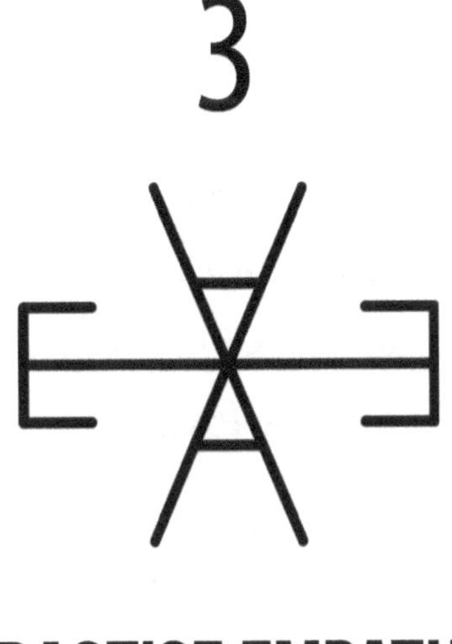

PRACTISE EMPATHY

Power-up score: 7

You can't understand someone until
you've walked a mile in their shoes.

1 CHOOSE

A robot cannot understand or practice empathy, yet.

Are you an empath, or do you sense how others
feel?

- Important because: you are not a robot. AI (Artificial Intelligence) and robots are coming to compete for your livelihood. Robots are already doing tasks once completed by humans. This is increasing because of its economic benefits to companies that require profit to grow. You are human. We are humans, and we have amazing capabilities that artificial intelligence and robots do not possess—yet. Right now we must strengthen our empathy for the sake of our future.

- Important because: you are a human. Humans are emotional sentient beings with a beautiful ability to sense, feel, and perceive things on a level that's ineffable or too great for words to describe. For example, I am writing this exact sentence right now. I am attempting to explain using the English language and words to describe a feeling. It's not even close. A word is simply a representation of a thing. Empathy is a thing that simply cannot be explained. It must be felt. It's visceral.

Gather as much relevant information about the other person. Ask questions or research using the internet. Once you have enough knowledge, close your eyes and imagine you are the other person. What are they thinking, feeling, seeing, doing and most importantly why? Humans have a wonderful ability of intuition. Knowing without having to fully understand. There will be an element of bias because you are unique and your perception of the world and others is specific to you. With practise you will become more adept at being empathetic. It will begin to change the way you connect with others. You'll experience less frustration, become calmer in social situations with new people and become more confident.

Did you know...

...a person diagnosed with antisocial personality disorder by the *Diagnostic and Statistical Manual of Mental Disorders (DSM–5)* of the American Psychiatric Association exhibits a lack of empathy, particularly an inability to feel remorse for one's actions. 'Many people with ASP do seem to lack a conscience, but not all of them,' he explains. Psychopaths always have this symptom, however, which is what makes them especially dangerous. 'When you don't experience remorse, you're kind of freed up to do anything—anything bad that comes to mind,' says Dr Black (https://www.health.com/mind-body/sociopath-traits).

I had a conversation via text message with my sister about empathy and the fact that I used to sense other people's feelings from a young age. But I didn't understand it then, and because it was too overwhelming, I possibly pushed it down into my subconscious mind to alleviate the overwhelm. It felt like I was feeling other people's pain or joy.

- Close your eyes and imagine what it's like to be somebody else for a day. Put yourself in their shoes. Who are you thinking of? Could it be a famous celebrity? Or an old schoolteacher or a boss you don't like? Now really think about who they are—their childhood, why they are who they are, and why they behave the way they do. How are you finding it? Difficult or easy? What did you learn?

- Next time you meet someone, focus on the nuances of their body language. What are the other person's eyes saying?

Empathy is a skill that can be developed over time. Being empathic makes you more valuable as a human in a heart-centred way and makes you potentially more employable compared to robots!

Empathy influences the science of mind and behaviour—psychology. It's what makes us a civilised collection of humans exhibiting kindness. For example, if you sense a child is frightened, you immediately comfort them by saying something reassuring: 'The spider won't hurt you, Jamie. It's probably more scared of you than you are of it' (unless it's an Australian funnel-web spider, then no!).

- Important because: collective empathy helps our progression as a species. If we are not empathetic of fellow humans, then we can become too selfish and insular. Have you ever heard someone say 'Ah, he's only out for himself, nobody else'? This behaviour is counterproductive.

- Important because: empathy reduces fear, because once you feel what other people are feeling, you become more compassionate. Compassion causes a lowering of fear. You are now focused on helping to actively remove suffering from others. How can you be fearful if you are helping others? What is there to fear?

Did you know... 'a specialised group of brain cells are responsible for compassion. These cells enable everyone to mirror emotions, to share another person's pain, fear, or joy' (Psychology Today, https://www.psychologytoday.com/au/blog/the-empaths-survival-guide/201703/the-science-behind-empathy-and-empaths).

I am an empath. This means my mirror neurons are highly sensitive. I felt this as a young child; however, it was too powerful to deal with, so as a psychological defence mechanism, I blocked it out. I pushed this amazing gift I had down into the depths of my psyche. I practically denied myself of my gift for many years. It was part of me. It is me. I've truly accepted it now. 'I am an empath.' Who resonates with this? After many, many years of personal development, overcoming pain and suffering—mainly severe depression and being hospitalised four times for mental illness—I built a rock-solid foundation of super-strong mental health. Now I embrace my power of empathy. My mirror neurons are stronger than ever. When I meet someone for the first time, I literally feel what they're feeling. Would you like to experience this? If yes, please keep reading.

- Next time you meet someone, take a moment to check what colour their eyes are. Why? The reason is that the two seconds it takes to do this allows time for you to really look into the other person's eyes. What this will do is amazing. By checking to see what colour their eyes are, you've focused purely on them. They will sense this. They will automatically feel your focus and attention. Who doesn't love attention? We are only human! Now enjoy that moment of connection when you both lock eyes for a moment. This is a basis for practising and building your empathy muscle.

- Notice two things about the other person's body language. First, their eyes. What do they look like? Wide open and still, or slightly squinting and shifty? Looking at you or beyond you? Make a mental note of the results. Now move on to their body. What are their hands and arms doing? Are they crossed and closed off, or are they open and welcoming? By simply focusing on these areas for now, you will grow your empathy muscle. Your mirror neurons will build in strength, like an arm muscle after consistent bicep curls at the gym. Now go practise!

Neurons that fire together wire together.
Hebb's Law

You are a human, yes? This means you have the capability for empathy. You'll build a strong foundation of psychological tools. Once you practise this, you'll be more valuable to the global marketplace. AI (artificial intelligence) and robots aren't going anywhere, and they will act as potential competition for work, jobs, and industries. You'll benefit psychologically and financially once you build your empathy muscle. Now go workout!

1 CHOOSE

- Important because: you'll feel the force and be empowered to feel what others are feeling. You'll become a stronger communicator and gain the ability to connect with others at a deeper level.
- Important because: once you practise empathy, you'll gain strength in sensing what other

people are feeling. You'll be more enlightened because your senses will be heightened to the next level. Did I hear you think 'sixth sense'? Hmmm, some call it intuition. I call it Jedi mind tricks master level!

Did you know that any time anyone in Star Wars is told 'Your thoughts betray you', their mind is being read? So be mindful and remember: you are not your thoughts. Thoughts are simply constructs of the mind.

My ability to empathise with others has improved, especially since experiencing depression. I was so focused on my own behaviour, thinking inwardly about myself, that I didn't notice others' behaviours. For example, my head would drop, with my shoulders hunched, and I literally didn't see other people's expressions. This meant it was difficult to connect with people, because I couldn't read them. I felt disconnected mentally and physically. It was draining. I was exhausted. Other people would see my depressed body language and either make a comment or shy away for fear of making things worse. It was a lose–lose situation that spiralled downwards.

- Physiology is key. Focus on other people's physiology. How are they standing? Upright or hunched over? Where are their eyes looking? Confidently at you or shifty? Once you focus on other people's body language, you'll gain valuable insight into their thoughts. How cool would this skill be? Plus, you will be less depressed because you'll start to mirror the other person. Therefore, you will become more connected. The human connection endorphins will fire up, and everyone in close proximity will be energised. Win–win.

- Make sure you practise your empathy skills regularly. Add a reminder to your calendar. If you're ambitious, add a daily reminder. If you're more conservative, add a weekly one. Either way, the consistency will build valuable empathy skills. For example: '1 April, 9.30 a.m. Walk into the office and look at the shoulders of Dave in Accounts. Slumped or upright?'

Knowledge is power. With respect to empathy, the more you focus on others, the more you'll learn and gather information that'll help you connect more deeply with people. It's a great thing! You'll start to feel so much better physically and mentally. Your mental health will power-up.

2 AWARENESS

Empathy with respect to our behaviour is important because using one or two simple and practical methods to increase your empathy is highly valuable, especially if practised daily.

- Important because: it heightens your awareness of both yourself and others.

- Important because: how can you feel what others are feeling if you aren't fully aware of what you're feeling within yourself?

Did you know great leaders can see and feel the potential in others, whereas poor leaders only see fault in others? Empathy is critical for great leadership.

(Please read Chapter 1, 'Choose Leadership', again if you feel or think it could serve you at this moment.)

In the past, as a growing boy, I used to feel what others felt. I'd feel sadness or happiness if I was near another human being, child or adult. These empathetic feelings overwhelmed me because I was too young to understand its gravitas. If anyone doesn't know what *gravitas* means, it refers to gravity or seriousness. To be honest, this word came to me without me intellectualising it. To share it with you clearly, I googled it! Classic googling behaviour. How did *google* become a verb? Anyway, I digress. Back to the point at hand. As a boy, because of the overwhelm of being an empath, I ignored this gift and strength. For years, I felt empathy for others in my own body, but I ignored it. In hindsight, this was a mistake. I now know the exponential power of empathy.

By listening to my body each and every time I feel empathy with another person, I acknowledge it. By doing this, it exercises my empathy muscle. And what happens when you work out a specific muscle? You get the picture!

- If you feel an emotion arise from seemingly nowhere when you're in close proximity with another person, simply acknowledge where it is in your body. Is it in your chest and heart or in your throat? By simply recognising and then accepting this beautiful human experience of empathy, you will build your empathy muscle.

Now write down what you took from this on a piece of paper, in your own words. Don't type it on your smartphone, because it doesn't have the same impact. You'll learn more in Chapter 7.

- Do you ever get a feeling or hunch that when you're with another person, whether a stranger or somebody you've known for a while, you know that they know that you know what they're thinking? That is empathy, my friend. Instead of discarding that moment, savour it and acknowledge it. Why? Because your empathy muscle will grow stronger. That's why. An added bonus is that you'll become more connected with that other person. If you've never felt that or you have no clue what I'm talking about here, with practice you will, I assure you. It's more of a feeling than a thought. It's more than intellectual; it's an emotion.

- Remember to know the importance of fully understanding the difference between empathy and sympathy, because they are completely different and have opposing outcomes.

Once you practise empathy, you will begin to build your empathy muscle. You'll become stronger each day as you continue to practise being empathetic.

Now go practise and have fun with it!

3 NOW

Three Challenges:

Pick one and commit taking action until you complete the challenge,

- Look someone in the eye for two seconds and imagine reading their mind.

- Next time you feel an emotion, acknowledge it and literally point to the part of your body where you're feeling it.

- If you feel empathy with another person, say 'Did you feel that?'

4

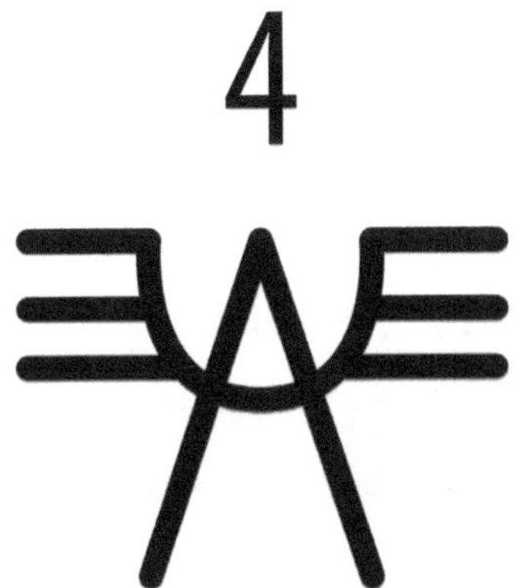

SELF-CARE-FULLY

Power-up score: 9

Self-carc is how you take your power back.
Lalah Delia

Sometimes the most important thing in a whole
day is the rest we take between two deep breaths.
Etty Hillesum

Almost everything will work again if you
unplug it for a few minutes, including you.
Anne Lamott

1 CHOOSE

When you care for yourself, you're really respecting yourself. For example, you can abuse your body through drugs, alcohol, cigarettes, and even food. Whatever you put into your mouth, it shows how much you respect your body, your machine. You only have one body. If you feed yourself with good-quality, nutritious, healthy food, it shows you're caring for your body and yourself with self-care, carefully. If you don't and you put loads of shit in your body, it shows you're not really caring for yourself. Therefore, you're not really showing yourself much respect.

This is one example where you may not be caring for yourself.

The first step is having awareness. Then you can start to make informed decisions about how you care for yourself.

What will you do today to show yourself you care? Please be mindful about caring for yourself, because you are the most important person right now. How can you look after someone else if you don't look after yourself first?

Self-care is how you treat yourself, and how you do this represents your self-worth.

- Important because: you cannot pour from an empty cup. How can you help others if you don't help yourself first?

- Important because: the level of your self-esteem is proportionate to the level of your confidence and ultimate success.

Did you know self-care reduces stress? Do you want to reduce stress? I thought so. Read on, my friend.

I used to think that doing something for myself first was selfish. For example, when I was younger and even if I was thirsty I wouldn't get a drink until I was offered one. Now, whenever I'm thirsty I immediately take action and get myself a drink. I also offer other's a drink too. This is an example of self-care and caring for yourself first because once you do you'll build your self-worth, self-leadership and acts of service for yourself and others.

- Be aware of how you talk to yourself, your internal and external dialogue. If you catch yourself saying 'I'm such an idiot', whether out loud or with your internal voice, stop, observe, and then know the truth. You are definitely not an idiot. If you keep saying it to yourself you may just start to believe it. This is certainly not helpful. Switch up your internal dialogue. For example, If you hear yourself, or others say "I'm an idiot" Call yourself out on it. Say "No you're not" The power of this practice becomes stronger with mindful repetition.

- Eat good-quality, wholesome, and healthy food. The more you do this, the better you'll feel within and without. You'll be respecting your body by giving it the highest-quality fuel. Your body is like a Ferrari, so it needs the best fuel. If you fill it up with poor quality fuel, the result is low performance. Meanwhile, if you give your body the best input, you'll have the best output. Your physical and mental performance will be so much better. So eat the good stuff! Eat lots of vegetables and fruits. I'm not saying deny yourself occasional treats as a reward, but make the best effort not to make it a regular habit, because ultimately, your body and mind will suffer. You have one body. Look after it, get it serviced regularly, and give it the best fuel; you'll be performing like a supercar in no time!

You are worthy of caring for yourself. Now practice self-care daily. It is not selfish. It could save your life. It will definitely change it for the better.

2 AWARENESS

Your mind and behaviour are affected by how you perceive and care for yourself, and your mental, emotional, and physical care is a high priority.

- Important because: you are important, and your self-care needs must come first, as it increases mood and well-being.

- Important because: you must be strong for yourself and within yourself before you can care for others. Practise regular self-care, and you will experience reduced anxiety.

Did you know that sleep deprivation will kill you quicker than food deprivation? 'Insufficient sleep deeply impairs our ability to consolidate and stabilize learning that occurs during the waking day' (*Harvard Business Review, https://hbr.org/2011/03/ sleep-is-more-important-than-f*).

I used to not care very well for myself. My sleep was disjointed, and I would berate myself for making mistakes. I'd literally call myself an idiot. This was evidently unhealthy, physically and psychologically. This was certainly a contributor to my spiralling into a deep depression. Lack of sleep caused me to become lethargic, irritable, and unmotivated. Self-deprecating language was picked up by my reticular activating system (RAS), which means I began to believe I was a lazy idiot. This was definitely not helpful for my mental health and well-being. Self-care is crucial to defend against toxic behaviours.

- Create a regular sleep routine by going to bed at the same time every night and waking up at the same time every morning.

- Check in with yourself daily. Ask yourself 'Hey, mate, how are you truly feeling today?' Then listen to your body and mind. Awareness is key. Adjust as necessary. Tired? Go to sleep a bit earlier. Irritated? Meditate for five minutes.

Practise self-care fully every single day by using positive language when thinking about yourself, being kind, and getting a good night's sleep most nights.

3 NOW

By repeating a positive self-care mantra to yourself you will eventually become a master of your mind.

- Important because whatever you regularly say to yourself either out loud or quietly and internally with your inside voice becomes who you believe you are.

- Important because your brain receives information in the form of knowledge that you choose to listen to.

Did you know self-care is a form of self-love and because there is only one you in the universe you must look after your 'spiritual' self by loving you.

- Allocate five minutes each day to practise looking after your spiritual self so that you build self-care and therefore self-love into your daily routine. Go for a walk or put your phone away. Be with yourself because you are great to be with!

- Write down one sentence about why you love yourself. For example, I am kind because I made a cup of tea for myself and my friend.

- Sip your drink and imagine the liquid gently falling down your throat and energising your whole body. Focus on the sensation of it nurturing you.

You can choose to practise mastery of your mind. Practise regularly and you'll become a master of self-care in no time. You will become a master of your mind. This is powerful.

How you carry yourself physically and mentally can affect your personal safety.

- Important because: criminals usually target people that appear helpless or powerless. For example, the way you walk to your car in a poorly lit street can determine if you're going to be approached or not.

- Important because: your mental state affects your level of environmental awareness. If you're less aware of what's happening around you, you're more likely to get injured or find yourself in a potentially dangerous situation.

Did you know that 'it takes a criminal just seven seconds to select their next victim? The criminals two biggest fears are getting hurt and getting caught. This knowledge empowers you in case you are picked.'

Sociologists Betty Grayson and Morris I. Stein conducted a study where they set up a video camera on a busy New York sidewalk and taped people walking by for three days.

The tape was later shown to inmates in a large East Coast prison who were incarcerated for violent offences (such as armed robbery, rape and murder) against people unknown to them.

Their key findings were that 'Every inmate chose exactly the same person, and the choices were not solely based on gender, race or age. Older, petite females were not automatically singled out. The inmates read the pedestrians' nonverbal signals and used those to make their choices' (https://www.nbcnews.com/better/health/seven-second-rule-how-avoid-being-seen-easy-target-ncna78922)

When I was a teenager I was walking with my friend at night and two guys were walking towards us. My friend happened to be looking down with his shoulders slightly hunched over. I was standing upright with squared shoulders and head up. Just as one of the guys approached us he took a swing a punched my friend in the face! Why do you think he did that? Apart from being a violent human he chose a victim that was easier to target.

- Adapt a powerful gait by walking assertively and confidently. Practise by walking at your own natural pace with your head up. Make each stride purposeful and powerful, with a clear sense of where you're going. Do your best to walk smoothly. Glide like a swan or do a Conor McGregor. I'm joking! To clarify, *gait* means 'the way a person walks'. I originally didn't know what it meant until I looked it up years ago. To be fair, it's not a word used regularly, is it?

- When you're out and about in the city, occasionally give people a quick bit of eye contact. This shows you're aware of your surroundings, and it alerts any would-be attacker, whether it's them you're looking at or not, that you're not going to be an easy target.

They way you walk can influence your level of confidence and how you're perceived by others, especially potential attackers. It could save you a trip to the hospital.

Three Challenges:

Pick one and commit.

- Meditate or do deep breathing for five minutes. (Start with thirty seconds.)

- Laugh heartily at least once a day. Watch your favourite comedy or share funny stories with friends.

- Get a full 8 hours sleep with no mobile phone or internet at night. Lights out!

5

EMBODY INTEGRITY

Power-up score: 8

Integrity is doing the right thing even when nobody's watching.

Doing the right thing is always the right thing to do.

1 CHOOSE

How you behave when nobody is watching is who you really are. Do you do the right thing by yourself and for yourself? By consistently doing what you know is best for you, you'll feel good about yourself now and in the future. So how do you know what's the right thing? You'll feel it. You'll instinctively know. If it feels not quite right, in a sense, that'll steer you in the right direction. It's about making the right choices that will serve you now. Also, your future self will thank you for it.

> The supreme quality for leadership is unquestionably integrity. Without it, no real success is possible, no matter whether it is on a section gang, a football field, in an army, or in an office.
> Dwight D. Eisenhower
> (https://www.inc.com/gordon-tredgold/31-reminders-of-the-importance-of-integrity.html)

Consistently doing the right thing by yourself and for yourself will serve you well now and in the future. It'll be a basis for living with authenticity and self-confidence.

- Important because: you'll be yourself wherever you are. Social anxiety will be reduced and eventually become non-existent. You'll become comfortable and relaxed in your own skin. You'll be confident in yourself at home and in public

- Important because: you'll have more energy because you'll be your true self whether in private or in public. There won't be all the switching between profiles because that gets tiring!

Did you know that the legendary Bob Marley once said, 'The greatness of a man is not in how much wealth he acquires, but in his integrity and his ability to affect those around him positively'? How does this make you feel?

For me, Bob Marley shared his feelings when he sang to the world:

> "One love,
> One heart,
> Let's get together and feel all right."

Before my beautiful son, Zachary, was born, I was a selfish man. I was egocentric, meaning I was all about me, myself, and I. As we discussed earlier, self-care is important. But if it's used as a means to only serve yourself, it's wasteful and selfish. Now I will share with you a poem I wrote in my amazing friend Kimberley Chakona's second book, *Poetry to the People*. It represents my feelings about fatherhood and how it powerfully encouraged me to ditch egocentricity and delve courageously and responsibly into altruism—living for others.

Here it is:

ANXIETY

Awake from disjointed slumber.
What is today? Another number?

The reflection of my frown hits back like profound emptiness mocking me from another dimension.
Stained sparingly with splatters of escaped toothpaste,
the bathroom mirror reveals a broken spirit.
Who is that sorry excuse of a man staring back from the stained glass?

This is going to be another long night.
The days are meaningless, should I fight?
Like a bolt of lightening anxiety hits.

With shallow breathing and pounding heart,
I am ready to drop I cannot cope.

Wave upon wave of visceral excitement flow through my body.
The 30th June 2014, a date etched in my soul forever.

As Mother Earth crouches painfully over the porcelain God, one contraction crowns a son.

A tear drops and feels like a tsunami.
This beautiful moment never forgotten.
Two souls bonded by unconditional love.
Knighted by fatherhood, past, future, and present become one.

This awe-inspiring soul created by love.

To a child, love is spelt 'time'.

- Doing the right thing is always the right thing to do - Be you, even when nobody's watching. It just feels right. Close your eyes and simply say your name out loud or internally. Say slowly and clearly "I am...[Name & Surname] then see what thoughts and feelings arise. This will start to create awareness and acknowledgement for who you are in this moment.

- Practice writing down an experience of how you are truly feeling in this moment. Use your own words and write as if nobody will read it except you. This will allow you a safe space that you've created to express your true feelings. It's not easy. It'll become easier with practice.

By practicing embodying integrity you will begin to become more comfortable in your own skin. You will start to really own who you are, It's an empowering practice that will grow stronger with regular practice. By doing what's right for who you are you will be more energised, more focused and you'll be open to liking who you are and who you are becoming. Self-love without arrogance will be the result. It's a great foundation for building rock-solid confidence.

2 AWARENESS

Once you embody integrity you will become happy with yourself and want the same for others.

- Important because we as human beings are social creatures that require relationships with others, and also with ourselves.

- Important because lasting happiness comes from within ourselves and not based on external things.

Did you know that the reality principle is viewing the world as it is, not as you want it to be?

I used to do things for others for approval thinking this was the right thing to do. Now I realise that doing things for others and myself without any need for the approval of others is the right thing to do no matter who is watching.

- Dance when nobody's watching because it frees you up to be yourself with yourself with no judgement. It may feel awkward. Do it anyway. It becomes easier as you become stronger. Try a few new moves!

- Dance like nobody's watching because you'll start to build confidence for not requiring any external approval for your choice of actions. Have you seen people dance without caring what others think?

Once you practice embodying integrity you will become stronger with who you are without needing external validation. This is massively freeing. It builds a strong foundation of lasting confidence across most situations.

3 NOW

Connecting your mind with your body with great respect to embodying integrity you will begin to join internal and external confidence.

- Important because you will create lasting and consistent balance between thinking and doing.

- Important because you will do what you say you'll do because it is the right thing to do

I used to think my mind was separate to my body. I categorised my thinking brain and mind as being its own entity and my body too. Now I realise they are one and the same. Interdependent and working in unison. Your brain controls your body and your body can influence your brain and mind.

- Pour yourself a glass of cool water. Place the glass on a table in front of you. Sit down a look at the water inside the glass. What do you see? Think about where the water will go once you drink it. What is its purpose? How is it connected to your body and mind? Now drink the water. Imagine the water traveling down your throat as it passes into your stomach. How long would your body and mind survive without water?

• Make yourself a cup of tea or coffee. Place the cup on a table in front of you. Sit down and watch the steam float into the atmosphere. Why is this happening?

By thinking about your daily habits with a sense of interconnectedness you will begin to realise the importance of mind-body connection with respect to integrity, by doing this regularly you will begin to train your body and mind to consider how your simple actions influence your behaviour. Most importantly how your behaviour is connected to others.

With respect to embodying integrity now, there are three things to focus on:

Number one is your behaviour.
Number two is virtue.
Number three is kindness.

Behaviour:

By being yourself, having integrity, and doing the right thing for yourself— by being you, simply being— it helps you control your behaviour. Controlling your behaviour is massively valuable. You will become a strong human being, simply being yourself and not being influenced externally by whichever society you happen to have been born into or whatever culture you're in. We have to respect society because you're part of it, and to be in this community, you need to abide by its laws and rules. However, you do not have to substitute or give up your integrity to live in this specific society. So be yourself.

Who are you?

Who are we?

How do you feel when you're truly being yourself?

I find that being myself regularly feels absolutely awesome. I'm embodying integrity and I am becoming aware of my behaviour. I still have a lot of work to do, because sometimes my behaviour does not represent me being who I am.

It's an influence; I've been influenced externally, and I let it affect my behaviour. So awareness is key.

Virtue.

Be virtuous, help others. Practise living in a way that will not hurt others and will not hurt you. Be a person of value and virtues. You are massively important. We all are. Once you understand this, not simply on an intellectual level but more on an emotional level and eventually a spiritual level, you will embody integrity, and you will be virtuous. Virtue will be a daily habit.

Kindness.

Humans are generally kind. Most people want to help others and be kind. Offer kindness and invite people in for a cup of tea or coffee into your home. Comfort others when they need it. Be charitable.

What does kindness mean to you?

Once you practise kindness, it's easier to be kind to others and share kindness, therefore embodying integrity by relating to your environment and others with great integrity, by practising and focusing on kindness and how you can be kind to others. Have you ever met anyone that was the complete opposite of kind and was potentially evil?

Why do you think that is? Perhaps they need more kindness. Perhaps they haven't been shown kindness. Perhaps they are not feeling kind towards themselves, so they project onto others. We all have the power to help ourselves and, in turn, to help others, and it comes from your mind. Our mind is not simply our brain. Our mind is how we interact with other environments using the tool of our brain. Connected to a nervous system, your mind is more than your brain. I take this teaching from KRS-One, Lawrence 'Kris' Parker (Knowledge Reigns Supreme). KRS-One said that when you close your eyes. What can you see?

I'm going to paraphrase this and create my own example:

Now close your eyes and imagine a 'green apple'.

Can you see a green apple?

How can you see this when your eyes are closed?

Now without moving your lips or creating any sound say 'green apple'

How did you say this without moving your lips?

Now hear yourself say 'green apple' without moving your lips or creating any sound with your voice.

Okay, how did you hear that without hearing any sound through your ears?

This is your mind. You may need to reread this page a few more times to fully grasp this powerful idea.

You can begin to become more aware of your mind to be kind, to be you, to control your behaviour.

Virtue. You're being virtuous in practising kindness. Also, you are not your thoughts. Thoughts are merely constructs of the mind, so don't feel bad or beat yourself up over thinking certain thoughts. They are not you; it is not your identity.
You can have integrity and embody integrity because you can control your behaviour. Your thoughts are not you. You are kind if you're virtuous and embody integrity and are aware of your behaviour. The solution to embodying integrity is this:

Think of ice cubes. So what I mean by that is, imagine you're in a work kitchen— a communal area, a community kitchen used by many people that you work with. Ice cubes are on the floor. You are the only one there. You could leave the ice cubes and get back to work and get on with your day. They will melt, and they will eventually dry up and disappear. The potential consequence of you leaving them could mean there could be a slipping hazard, for example.

The message is:

Don't walk over the ice cubes.

Take action, have integrity, and clean up the ice cubes simply because you want to clean up the ice cubes. More importantly you choose to pick up the ice cubes.
It won't take long to pick them up and dry them. Dry the floor area and then get on with your day, with integrity.
Remember, it's an analogy. There are many ice cubes, so to speak, in the world as you go about your day.
Don't walk over ice cubes.

You will become a greater person, a greater human. Remember to dance when nobody is watching.

You are gently becoming a master of the mind. On your own, dance with your eyes closed if you want to. Make sure there are no sharp edges close by. Safety first!

Put some music on, your favourite music, and dance like nobody's watching.

It might feel a bit awkward to start with, but when you become comfortable in your own body, being yourself, It will be empowering. You'll feel energised. So dance. Dance like nobody's watching. When will you be dancing?

Love. Love. Love.

Love conquers all.

When you love yourself, all matter matters. And thinking about love intellectually is one thing. For example, what is love? What is the word *love*?

What does it represent?

There are many descriptions of love, and you can think about it intellectually. However, one is you really feel it emotionally in your heart. Connected to who you are, with respect to your behaviours, your virtue, and your kindness.

In practising various methods to embody integrity, you will start to understand and overstand love. Love is more than intellectualising it. It surpasses superficial thought and into a deeper level of being, of being you. How do you create this higher level? A stronger emotion. A loving emotion? Love is probably the most powerful energy created by us. Can you encourage it by moving your body?

By simply moving your body and creating emotion by cleaning up the ice cubes and dancing like nobody's watching, you will feel love for yourself. Therefore, you will be in an awesome position to love others.

How beautiful is that?

By practicing being an effective human being with integrity will build your character.

- Important because it will simplify your life and reduce complexities prevalent in modern living

- Important because it will encourage trust to be built with yourself and for others

Did you know that people with integrity are more successful, decisive, trustworthy, and make better leaders with stronger relationships?

As a young child I used to occasionally do the wrong thing. It never felt quite right. For example, if my mother or father kindly asked me "Did you do your homework" I'd lie and say: "Yes!" Why would I do that? In hindsight, I realise that breaking trust with people that love me is one of the worst conscious decisions I could have made. By choosing not to embody integrity in that moment I'd cheated myself of doing what's right for me. The consequences of my actions could have burned relationships. Thankfully we grow from children into adults and I'm grateful for the lessons I've learnt and still learning. We all must live with our decisions and the consequences when it comes to our integrity.

- When you are deciding to take action and it doesn't feel quite right. Listen to this feeling because it's telling you something important. Then choose how to proceed. What will you decide and why?

- Think: How would I feel if someone did this to my grandmother? Then proceed with your choice. What will you decide and why?

Doing the right thing is always the right thing to do.

Do it.

Three Challenges:

1. Consolidate your values into three core values by asking yourself "What 3 things are most important to me when it comes to doing the right thing in all my daily actions?" For example - Kindness, service, trust.
2. Do not lie for 24 hours. Zero lies, untruths or fibs.
3. Research: 'What is Stoicism?' by googling it and pick one phrase you find that strongly resonates with you. Write it down.

Pick one and commit.

6

LEVERAGE LANGUAGE

Power-Up Score: 6

Words have energy and power with the
ability to help, to heal, to hinder, to hurt,
to harm, to humiliate, and to humble
Yehuda Berg

1 CHOOSE

Three benefits of leveraging language:

ONE

Improving meaning in your life and in your interactions with others, increasing focus on what is most important to you.

- By leveraging language, you increase your level of awareness of other people and of yourself.

- By understanding what language is and how it represents meaning by using words you will develop refined communication skills. You will better understand, and be understood by others.

- Psychologically, it is beneficial to have an acute awareness of what your environment means to you and what it means to others.

TWO

You increase your knowledge and understanding of yourself, of others, and of your environment, so your psychology emphasises and increases in knowledge by learning new things specifically related to how you understand language and the system of language.

- It can help you begin to increase your understanding of other people and their behaviours, why they do what they do, and the meaning surrounding it, with respect to language, by increasing knowledge. Therefore, beginning to understand and increasing understanding leads to wisdom.

THREE

Your mind will be sharper, quicker and with more agility.

- Your mind will be more effective, and your thinking skills will improve. You can start to utilise the system of language. For example, Chomsky's L.A.D (Language Acquisition Device) How do we absorb language and knowledge?

  'A language is not just words. It's a culture, a tradition, a unification of a community, a whole history that creates what a community is. It's all embodied in a language.' Noam Chomsky

Three solutions for leveraging language:

ONE

Look up words you don't know. If you see a word in a sentence, simply google it. Look it up. Read the definitions and then google the synonyms of it.

- Look up at least three similar words because you'll increase your understanding of words and how they're a part of language. It will improve how you understand meaning.

TWO

Focus on body language. Did you know 80 percent of communication is non-verbal? So focusing on body language will improve your skills, with respect to leveraging language psychologically.

- Focus on what people are doing with their arms. Are their arms crossed? Are their arms open?

- People talk with their bodies. Really start to listen to what other people's body language is saying.

THREE

Practise mirroring. When you mirror somebody, you gently copy what they're doing. So if they're crossing their arms, gently cross your arms too. If they're leaning against the wall, gently lean against the wall too.

- It creates a sense of unity and similarity, which will improve your connection with them and your understanding of others.

7

SIMPLIFY FOCUS

Power-Up Score: 6

The greatest weapon against stress is our
ability to choose one thought over another.
William James

1 CHOOSE

Building confidence and moving from low confidence
to super-strong mental health must be simplified.

Create stillness of the mind.

- Creating stillness of the mind is a great tool that you can use to effectively change and develop how you think. If you had a nail you could do certain things with it. But, without a hammer, it'll be very difficult to do what you need to do, even though you wanted to. Once you get the right tools, like a hammer to hammer the nail in effectively, you will be able to build what you want to build a lot more effectively than when you don't have the tools.

- When creating stillness of mind, building your mindset is greater once you are aware of how you relate to your environment in the world and how we relate to other people. Having greater awareness helps us navigate life fluidly instead of fighting against it. Being aware means that you can make confident decisions based on the available stimulus with respect to psychology.

What is entering your mind through your ears, through your eyes, and through all the senses?

Once you become aware, you will be more confident, and be in a stronger state to practice emotional control. How great would it be for you to be able to control your emotions in any situation? Having emotional control helps you and others to influence situations. Most importantly, to firstly influence yourself to have emotional control. Because if you lose control of your emotions, you lose control, and if you lose control in certain situations, it can be potentially dangerous, potentially life-threatening, and can affect your life in the future. So the benefits of creating stillness of the mind help improve your emotional control, which will help you to be massively confident and live an awesome life.

Use your 'mind tools' in various environments. 'Be the hammer'. For example, think of how you're absorbing information everyday. The RAS (Reticular Activating System) is a network in the human brain that helps you filter relevant stimulus and information so that your brain can handle and processes the massive amounts of data entering the brain. With great respect to where you want to go in life and who you want to become, once you are mindful by creating a stillness of mind, you can utilise your brain to be more effective by focusing on what's important to you at any given moment.

I was in a restaurant, and my focus was on listening to my friend. They were going through a tough time, and I wanted to concentrate on listening to their story, to what has been going on with them. I really focused on the sound of their voice. The words they were speaking from their mouth were entering my ears. I was holding on to every word. This focus improves retention, improves listening skills, and improves understanding of your friends and people close to you. People important to you.

What are the important mind tools, environments and situations, you think could help you focus on one sense at a time?

First, focus on your eyes. What are you seeing?

Then focus on your ears. What are you hearing? What sounds are coming into your ears?

And so on, through every sense.

Focus on your mouth, What you are tasting?
Focus on your skin. What you are touching?
Focus on your nose. What you are smelling.?
So you have sight, touch, taste, hearing, and smell.

8

COMMIT TO LIFELONG LEARNING

Power-Up score: 8

An investment in knowledge pays the best interest.
Benjamin Franklin

Did you know adopting a growth
mindset creates a passion for learning
rather than a hunger for approval?
Carol Dweck

I know that I know nothing.
Socrates

1 CHOOSE

You don't know what you don't know.

Repetition is the mother of skill.

Learning how to learn better builds knowledge and wisdom therefore creating intrinsic motivation for lifelong learning.

- Important because we don't know what we don't know. Once you know you know, you know? By learning something new we build confidence because our understanding deepens. Like plant roots growing longer and stronger as it receives water and light.

- Important because you'll be more effective at processing information which means you'll acquire skills. Developing skills will increase your confidence because you'll grow competence in new arenas. Gladiators that held the highest skills were more likely to triumph after confidently stepping into the arena. Round one. Fight!

Did you know that a 'gladiator' in ancient Rome comes from the Latin word 'gladius' which means sword?

When I first started skateboarding as a child I could not perform the most technical basic trick, the ollie. I would excitedly watch the older boys execute huge ollie's and land flawlessly. I was in awe! I remember thinking 'how do they do that?' In hindsight I realised that the question is the answer. Radley, a local skateboarder kindly showed me the mechanics of an ollie. He broke it down into three simple steps to explain how to do an ollie. Step one, tap the tail of the skateboard. Step two, slide your front foot up towards the nose. Step three, jump. Now, I can confidently say that since I started skateboarding many moons ago and have performed thousands upon thousands of ollie's. I love the process of learning and applying new skills to have fun! Now it's your turn. What will you decide to learn next?

- Adopt a 'growth mindset' so that you learn to become intrinsically motivated to learn for the sake of learning.

- To start to adopt a growth mindset when facing any problem start saying: "I don't know how to do this, yet". Yet' is the most important word here because humans have an ability to learn almost anything. Remember this every day by including this word in your language.

By adopting a growth mindset you will begin to shift from extrinsic to intrinsic motivation to learn. You will then be in a powerful position to commit to lifelong learning.

2 AWARENESS

Consistently acquiring knowledge is important in building long-term confidence. Do you want to be confident everyday?

- Important because competence strengthens as a result of learning new skills.

- Important because with increased competence comes greater confidence.

Did you know that reading regularly makes you smarter because you're more likely to learn something new and it helps you retain knowledge?

- Pick a book, any book, and start reading. Set a timer and read for 5 minutes non-stop. If you'd prefer online reading perhaps download a reading app. I use a great app called 'Blinkist'. It summarises key concepts of non-fiction books into chunks or 'blinks'

- Pick a hobby, any hobby, and start doing it. What's most important is starting and making sure you adopt a growth mindset, meaning you will fail and that's ok. It's positively encouraged because it's the fastest way to learn quickly from your mistakes. Think intelligently about what you will change to now that you know what doesn't work.

- Pick a coach or mentor that has experience and results in what you're keen to learn. They'll teach and guide you more effectively than if you tried to be self-taught. That's ok too if that's your choice. Although being coached or mentored will save you valuable time. Time is more valuable than money. You can always make more money but you can never make more time.

Become a reader because your brain will be exercised and your mind will become sharper. Start a new hobby. The more challenging the better! Getting out of your comfort zone is great for building your resilience and you'll become a stronger and faster learner. Seek guidance from people that have walked the walk and have the scars, metaphorically or literally, to prove it. You'll be loving learning in no time. By learning new skills, building on knowledge and progressing from competence to excellence you will be bursting with confidence. It's massively energising! Do you want more energy?

3 NOW

Learning how to meditate will build you a stronger brain, for your lifetime. The time of your life.

- Important because your 'mind muscle' will become more agile with a stronger ability to apply knowledge for wisdom. You'll be a good problem-solver with a powerful ability to navigate life. Some call it 'adulting'

- Important because you'll develop the skill to remain calm in potentially stressful situations. This is particularly important as you gain more responsibility as life, and time progresses forward. Just got fired from work? No big deal. The kids are screaming? Piece of cake! Car got stolen. Fine! Equanimity and peace of mind will be yours all because you practice daily meditation.

Did you know that meditating increases gamma waves leading to neuroplasticity? This is the brain's ability to change functionally depending on environmental input.

In the past I never used to meditate. I knew there were some benefits but after attempting it a few times I pretty much gave up because it was too difficult and I didn't see immediate results. This was before becoming ill. Seriously ill, mentally. Since then I knew I had to succeed. So I persevered with my practice of meditation. I realised that expecting a result after a few attempts was like going to the gym twice and expecting to gain six pack abdominal muscles! Now I meditate every single day without fail for nine minutes. Now, I feel agile in mind, my thoughts are sharper and I sleep better and I am more creative, with abundant energy.

- Start small. For example, close your eyes and breathe in for three seconds and breathe out for three seconds. Repeat three times. What's most important is starting. If you decide you want to go to the gym, most of us know the hardest part is actually getting there. Once we arrive it's much simpler to carry on.

- Make sure you commit to your meditation practice consistently, in whatever capacity suits you, for at least three weeks. For example, even one minute of meditation repeated daily for three weeks is better than nothing.

The powerful and mentally healthy habit of regular meditation will result in you building your brain strength and power. You will become strong in mind because after three weeks your practice will become an ingrained habit. You will certainly start to feel the results. Let me know how you go.

In addition, you will increase the neuroplasticity of your brain resulting in 'restoring old, lost connections and functions that have not been used in some time, enhance memory, and even enhance overall cognitive skills' (positivepsychology.com/neuroplasticity)

Adopt a growth mindset to all aspects of your life.

- Important because you will become stronger and more confident in your ability to rise after falling, so to speak. You will no longer fear failure because you will understand the importance of this powerful word: 'Yet'. For example, I don't know how to do a kickflip on a skateboard, yet.

- Important because you will start to reframe and retrain your brain to approach every challenge in life as a great learning opportunity. You will begin to actively look for challenges to overcome because you know that even if you fail. You will fail forward and learn from it. You will be confident in knowing you will always progress by adopting a powerful growth mindset.

Did you know that a 'growth mindset is based on the belief that your basic qualities are things you can cultivate through your efforts' (Carol Dweck)

When I was growing up I used to think that the smart kids were just smart because they were born that way. I thought, incorrectly, that it was just how it was and I had to accept that I just wasn't as smart as the kids that got high test scores consistently. Now, I know that that was simply a fear I had. A fear of failing. A false fear that I wasn't good enough and that I would never be able to get the highest grades. This attitude and pervasive way of thinking highlighted the reason I didn't get the results I wanted was because I didn't think I could, or that I didn't deserve them. But, with a growth mindset I now know that it's just because I have not learnt how to, yet. Who can land kickflips now? Me, that who! Stoked.

- Once you realise that F.E.A.R is False Evidence Appearing Real. You will begin to put your hand up for opportunities that you may have previously not attempted for fear of failure. With a growth mindset and attitude that failure is ok and it's a learning opportunity you will always progress. Whatever you choose to do make sure you always adopt a growth mindset because you will become a champion. A champion of your thoughts. Most importantly your actions.

- By adding an extra dose of effort into whatever you choose to do will have a big impact on the trajectory of your life. In work, in your relationships, in anything you decide you want to get good at. For example, in a job interview, prepare for an extra thirty minutes. To be the best you can be. To be great. It starts with a choice to adopt a growth mindset.

By adopting a powerful growth mindset you will be empowered to harness the power of 'yet'. You will take that risk and attempt any challenge you want because you know that to be the best you must put in the effort. You must not give in to any F.E.A.R of failure because you know that you will learn and fail forward. Be patient with this and your confidence will skyrocket. Boom!

Three Challenges:

1. Start a new hobby. Any hobby. For example, learning to play the saxophone or how to surf.
2. Volunteer to help someone complete a task without being asked (even if you don't have the skills, *yet*)
3. Visualise yourself being the best in the world at something, anything. For example, imagine you have just become a Formula one racing car champion. You've just beaten Lewis Hamilton. How do you feel?

Pick one and commit.

Have fun with these challenges!

SHARE KNOWLEDGE

9 is my favourite number. It
resonates with me. Why?

Power-Up Score: 7

By sharing knowledge you each learn one
another's ideas and you come up with new ones.
Vivek

Sharing is caring.

We are greater than the sum of our parts: 1 + 1 = 3

Teamwork = The Collective Mind

1 CHOOSE

Always be learning and once competent with whatever you've learned, share this knowledge with others. Ensure you ask permission first or it could get a bit annoying for others! Avoid being known as the know-it-all.

- Important because cognitive plasticity is valuable. The benefits of continuous learning are that it reduces the likelihood of developing dementia in our later years. It increases the sharpness and flexibility of your mind.

Did you know your brain is 3 percent of your body weight but needs 30 percent of the blood supply?

In the past I wasn't focused on learning every day. It was as if I was forced to by going to school. I used to play around, be a little bit naughty, and doodle, and I was not really interested in structured learning. Then I found skateboarding. Now I was focused. My mind and brain was like a sponge, absorbing all the knowledge required to learn the foundational tricks needed to progress my skills in skateboarding. I loved it; it gave me massive energy. So find your focus, what will encourage you and initiate you into wanting to learn every day, compared to being forced to learn every day.

Ask why?

Be curious. Make your brain exercise by asking why.

Why does the sun rise?

Why is it cold in winter?

Why, why, why.

- Research valid sources. To be discerning of the knowledge you are learning. Do these sources have credibility? Do the people have the necessary skills? Are they believable? Why? Discernment is important.

Practise lifelong learning. Always be learning.

Cognitive plasticity is great for your psychology, your mind, and your behaviour. It reduces the likelihood of dementia. It increases the agility of your brain and strengthens your mind. By asking why and researching these sources, you will have a stronger and healthier brain and mind.

2 AWARENESS

Keep an eye on your mind with respect to sharing knowledge.

- Important because by focusing on your brain and mind connection, you will improve your mind power.

- Important because by sharing knowledge with others you'll gain higher skills in your base knowledge. Simply by teaching others what you know you will reach mastery of your skills faster. In the process of sharing skills with others you become more refined in skill. Plus it can be extremely rewarding when you witness someone experiencing that 'Eureka!' moment. You being the catalyst for another person learning and enjoying learning is fulfilling. Plus as a side benefit you build confidence. Fantastic!

Practise it.

Live it.

Do it every day.

The benefit is that knowledge is power. What you do with that power is your choice. Knowledge is a great opportunity to learn and apply the learning. With respect to your brain–mind connection and awareness, in practising living it and doing it, with respect to knowledge, the benefit is, it will increase your energy. Learning excites the mind by purely being a human being. Your brainpower will be strengthened by learning, by practising, by living, and by doing.

Pick a topic, any topic you like. I particularly enjoy learning about quantum mechanics. What do you like to learn about?

Did you know your brain's storage capacity is almost unlimited? My brain and my mind—in the past, I used to think that they were separate. I used to think that my brain was one thing and my mind was another. This is where Jedi mind awareness comes into play. Your brain is a tool. It's a muscle that you use. You can utilise the tool, the organ of your brain, and you can play the music if you understand and know how to play its chords. On the other hand, your mind—what is your mind?

Is it your mind?
Is it our mind?

Close your eyes for one moment. Cover your ears too. Say out loud 'NOW' without opening your mouth and without opening your eyes and with your ears covered.

What did you hear?
Who created that?
Who said 'NOW'?

And how is it you can hear it without saying a word and without the use of your ears, as they were covered? Your brain and your mind and the sound have you saying the word *NOW* without using your voice. That is our mind. It is all part of the same system. What is that system?

As above, so below.

The solution is do and undo.

Lifelong learning with respect to being in the 'NOW' You must do. Practise it, live it, do it. You must learn how to play the organ of your brain in the system of our minds. Practising this valuable lesson and behaviour creates awareness every single day

Be like a sponge. Absorb knowledge with a discernment filter. The words that are spoken or sung and the music that is composed and performed are all rich forms of information. Some more credible and useful than others. Be discerning about which voice and songs you listen to.

'Music is the one incorporeal entrance into the higher world of knowledge which comprehends mankind but which mankind cannot comprehend' - Ludwig Van Beethoven

'Do. Or do not. There is no try' - Yoda. A Jedi Master

So the brain–mind connection with respect to being in the 'now' is practise it and do it. Knowledge is power. You will increase your brainpower and energy. Your brain storage capacity is almost unlimited. Always be learning.

3 NOW

Share knowledge and give it away to develop and to contribute to the progression of global knowledge. The benefits of that is, you will develop refined knowledge, from general towards more specific depth of knowledge, as opposed to shallow knowledge purely focused on description.

You will begin to create clarity—
depth and clarity of knowledge—
which is exemplified by understanding and simplifying the language used to share knowledge with others.

Did you know your brain is like a muscle? The more you exercise it by learning, sharing, explaining and teaching concepts, ideas, and how to do certain things, the more you will build your brain muscle; it will strengthen.

Why is sharing knowledge a good thing? I used to keep my knowledge to myself. Why did I do that? Perhaps it's because I didn't feel confident sharing what I knew. With depth and with clarity of the knowledge I have now, I do my best to share as much knowledge with others, with confidence. With respect to what they choose to listen to, I do my best to request permission to share my knowledge first as common courtesy.

The solution is to contribute to a discussion and add value. You are likely to know something and have knowledge of a particular area more than somebody else in a conversation. It's likely. Remember that and add to the discussion. Contribute your knowledge and add value. If they didn't know the knowledge you share and contribute, the other party, the other people in the conversation, will be grateful. And if they, in fact, already know what you know, it will create a common bond, which is a benefit to the discussion. So in the future, remember this. Also, ask permission before offering knowledge or advice, because it will help your listener accept what you are saying and be open to it, as opposed to shutting down because you didn't ask them for permission first.

So share knowledge, because growth will happen once you do this every day.

10

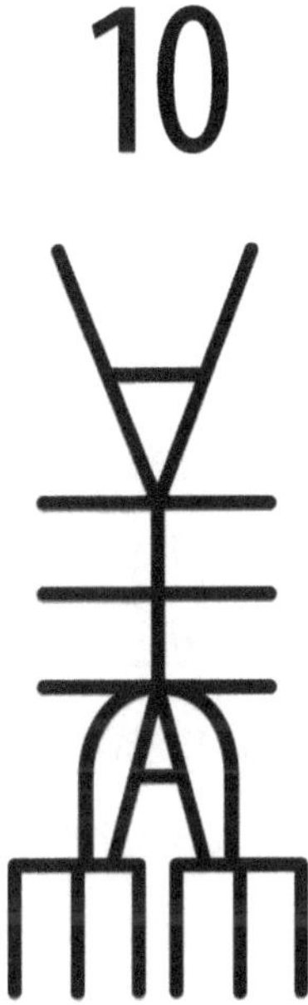

RELEASE CREATIVITY

Power-Up Score: 9

Imagination is more important than knowledge.
Einstein

There is no innovation and
creativity without failure.
Brené Brown

Art, freedom and creativity will change
society faster than politics.
Victor Pinchuk

1 CHOOSE
Release creativity confidently

Releasing creativity empowers you to shift from consumer to creator.

Once you begin to create value you will begin exchanging this value for money. It's a resource to use as you choose. We could all dedicate more energy to increase our creativity, because humans need to create things. It's part of human nature; it's part of who we are.

Did you know that daydreaming provides a mental incubation period, enhancing creative thinking, long-term planning, and self-awareness?

I used to daydream regularly when I was younger. My mind would wander. I imagined scenarios that were so much fun. But I felt guilty because I was supposed to be in reality when I was imagining and creating, daydreaming in my mind. Being guilty is a waste of your mental resources, I have found. Now without any guilt, with confidence, and in the excitement, I regularly daydream. Daydreaming is a way to practise releasing creativity. Let your mind wander.

Schedule regular daydreaming sessions every single day, and you'll start to discover how creative you really are. Then write down what you daydream about. This way, you will start to practise releasing your creativity, therefore empowering you to shift from consumer to creator. You'll start to imagine and use your powerful imagination to think of ideas, new ideas that could provide great value to yourself and other people. Personally and commercially.

Also, focus on your five senses whilst daydreaming. Touch, taste, smell, sight, hearing. So in turn think about at least two things connected to each sense.

For example, touch two things nearby. It could be a cup of water. It could be a pen. Then move to taste. Drink a glass of water and taste a juicy green apple. Then smell what two things your sense of smell detects. Now sight. What things immediately draw your eyes' attention? Hearing. What two things are you hearing right now?

In conclusion, you are releasing creativity by scheduling daydreaming sessions and focusing on your five senses and not being guilty about daydreaming. You'll provide your imaginative mind and your powerful unlimited imagination with an important incubation period, therefore releasing creativity and empowering you to shift from consumer to creator.

You will create.
You are creative.

You'll be able to create value, which can be exchanged for money. Have you ever thought about starting your own business? Think of the possibilities!

2 AWARENESS

Releasing creativity is a critical part of building confidence with respect to your psychology. Confidence and psychology relates strongly to creativity. Being creative and practising creativity in releasing your creative potential is hugely beneficial to building confidence and creating value in your life and in other people's lives, for your lifestyle and also for business and commercial aspects too. So there are definitely benefits to releasing your creativity.

Biopsychology is a part of psychology that focuses and stems from the brain and biological sections and ideas and frameworks with respect to psychology. Releasing creativity through tried-and-tested methods of neuroscience and behavioural neuroscience which adds scientific weight to your neurophysiology, your brain system, your thinking, and various molecular structures in your brain, and how that relates to your creativity. Also, another benefit of releasing creativity is a focus on your RAS. It's your reticular activating system.

It's a filter in your brain that filters all extraneous stimulus and information, because there are millions of bits of information vying for your attention as you go about your day. Your brain simply cannot handle all the information out there. So the reticular activating system acts as a set of, let's say, traffic lights. It lets in certain bit of information, to be processed in your brain. So green light in, red light out. For example, you're walking down the street, and there's lots going on in the busy outside shopping mall or high street. There's lots of different noises, people talking, a helicopter going past, lots of advertising lights, and flashing cars going past.

What your reticular activating system does is, it filters out all the other bits of information. This will be focusing on absorbing the relevant information at the time. For example, to keep you safe and make sure you're not walking out into the street, you can hear cars and a wealth of other important information. So with releasing creativity with respect to psychology and neuroscience, there are certain solutions that can help you as a strategy to improve your creativity. Before we do that, I will let you in on a few secrets of nature to give you a contrast of the reticular activating system in humans and then in nature. Have you heard of the mantis shrimp? It is an absolutely magnificent creature. Why? Because compared to humans, what it can do is, it can absorb thousands and thousands of pieces of information all at once into its brain without processing it first, compared to humans, where with the reticular activating system we have, we can only process maybe one or two pieces of information at once before it gets absorbed into the brain. Conversely, the mantis shrimp can, without processing, absorb hundreds, if not thousands, of pieces of data at once. An amazing creature.

How do we improve our creativity? How do you practise creativity, and how do we release creativity, most importantly to build confidence?

Number one: Language.

Your language is massively important in creating creativity. How is language? What comes out of your mouth, the words, phrases, the tone— all have an effect and influence on your creativity and therefore your confidence.

The words you use are a representation of your thought processes, and if you use terms like 'I'm an idiot', that acts as a command to your brain, to your mind. Through the reticular activating system, it's filtered into your brain as a command.
And with that language, 'I am an idiot', you'll start to believe it, and with repetition, that can have damaging effects on your confidence, on your creativity, on your emotional state, and on your physical state. So your language is massively important.

Be mindful of what language you use. Ask people to keep you accountable for what language you use with yourself and with others. Reframe your language. Use positive language—for example, 'I am intelligent. I am intelligent. I am intelligent.' Repeat it. Repetition is the mother of skill, so repeat, repeat, repeat the language you use. It is massively important to building creativity.

Number two: Physiology.

How you use your body affects your creativity in your mind. If you feel tired, for example, you can, in fact, kick tiredness by literally jumping, performing ten star jumps. Get your heart pumping, get your body moving, and it changes your mindset. It changes your body and psychology, and it changes you by adjusting your physiology. By jumping up and down, for example, that will create energy in your mind, and the amount of energy that you can release is incredible, beyond what you think. For example, if you say 'I am a marathon runner. I commit to running a marathon.' Usually, 99 percent of people who say 'I commit to running a marathon' do it. They actually do it. And physiology for starting to run, starting to jump up and down, it trains your mind to release energy to be focused on what you need to do. So instead of it coming from your mind first, it comes from your physiology first, which is strong.

Focus on your language, your physiology, your reticular activating system, and your mindset changes your state so you can go from an apparent tiredness to massive energy. All that it takes is a little switch in your physiology and having focus on your language, and this all helps release creativity, release energy, and most importantly, build confidence—a great foundation of confidence. And did you know that people who are open to new experiences are more creative than others who are not?

Be open to new experiences. If someone asked you 'Would you like to go for a run?' and your immediate thought was 'No, I'm not a runner', how about giving it a go? You could even start with a short walk. It will change your physiology, it will change your state, and there are massive benefits to it. You might even have your million-dollar idea while still running.

Also, did you know that loss and trauma can have creative effects? If your mindset is one of gratitude for having loss and trauma in your life, it shifts your perspective on your life. It's called post-traumatic growth. Building resilience and ultimately confidence in the process.

3 NOW

Less is more.

- Important because releasing creativity doesn't have to always be adding things. By doing less and removing or omitting things, you help to simplify your creativity. Being mindful of this will help your unique creative process now and into the future. It will reduce any perceived pressure to add extra. So, less is more.

- Important because 'simplicity is the ultimate sophistication' Doing nothing can sometimes be the best course of action. Do less.

Did you know that by focusing on less you increase clarity. Clarity is power.

I used to overthink. I still do a bit. I am definitely improving. But, once I began to simplify my ideas I'd become more confident in executing them and making my creations a reality. I've written this book!

- Do less

Your confidence will undoubtedly grow by releasing creativity and doing less, with clarity and focus.

The problem is not being creative or not practising creativity. How creative do you think or feel you are?

Why is this so?

The benefits to releasing creativity in practising improving your creativity is that it improves your problem-solving skills. It increases the value that you create in the world, in the marketplace, in business and employment, and in commercial aspects as well as personal development. Most importantly, releasing creativity increases confidence massively, and confidence is key to almost everything in life. So with problem-solving, you're taking a problem, analysing it, and getting creative with a solution. And solutions are massively valuable, because everyone has problems. People, families, relationships, businesses—there are always problems to solve, and being able to create a solution is an excellent thing. Having value, creating value out of your mind, out of what you do, out of your behaviours, out of your decisions. Creating value by being creative will stand you in great stead for building an awesome future for yourself and your family and your friends and, for whether you want or need confidence, building confidence.

How do you feel when you witness someone else that has great confidence?

We all know that there's a fine line between confidence and arrogance. What's the difference?

Between confidence and arrogance, what would you prefer to have?

So being creative increases confidence. What are the solutions? Before we get to the solutions, there's a fact about creativity. Studies have been done that concluded that 80% of people have their creative thoughts and ideas when having a shower. So next time you're having a shower, have a think about an idea, or if you have an idea if you're in the shower, write it down.

Solutions. So number one:

Create habits, daily habits that will improve the likelihood of you getting into a great habit of being creative and practising creativity, where you don't even have to think about it. For example, going back to the shower, every time you have a shower, but taking a notepad not into the shower, it'll get wet! Put it out to the side so that it prompts you to get your creative juices flowing. Once you've repeated this for about two weeks you'll develop a habit that sticks. It'll be like brushing your teeth daily, we can start to create a great habit. I've been creative by putting that trigger in place, whether it's putting out a pen and pencil and pad down by the side of your bed or in the bathroom before you have a shower or before you go to sleep creates that trigger. So start to get into a great habit of being creative.

Are you an introvert?

If so, there are definitely benefits of introversion. For example, introverts get de-energised or tired all the time from being around lots of people. Introverts generally need a bit of solitude, with time on their own, to re-energise. This solitude creates a space for creativity, so having that time alone is a great thing, whether you're an introvert, an extrovert, or ambivert, like me (I'm a mix of both introversion and extroversion). So create a habit and schedule in some time for solitude. Schedule in, say, for example, 7 a.m. to 8 a.m. That is your schedule on Monday to Friday, or even depending on your time, for your life situation or family situation, set aside half an hour or an hour every weekend too. Practise solitude and creativity. Make sure you schedule it. It's highly likely to happen, because what gets scheduled gets done.

Another solution is reading. Read with depth and variety. I highly recommend reading non-fiction books. It's completely up to you though. That's my preference, because I believe non-fiction books are more valuable, with respect to creativity and building confidence. With regard to confidence psychology, reading helps put knowledge into your mind, into your brain. The more you read, the more knowledge your brain has. The more words, concepts, ideas, paradigms, and frameworks, the higher the likelihood you will create magnificent things, because you'll have that framework, you'll have an idea, you'll have the knowledge.

Creativity is building something, creating something, linking two initially disconnected ideas or thoughts into one. So creating something new, something innovative, something imaginative from your imagination. Being creative by linking two separate ideas or items from your mind together to create something completely brand new and innovative.

So will you do some reading, now? [You are right NOW]

Three Challenges:

Pick one and commit.

1. Read a book in 7 days (It could be this one)
2. Do some free-writing. Grab the nearest pen. Now set your timer for 5 minutes and write nonstop until the time is up. Your theme is: Confidence
3. Do some free-drawing. Grab the closest pencil, or pen. Now set your timer for 5 minutes and draw nonstop until the time is up. your theme is: Space

11

SOCIALISE INFLUENCE

Power-Up Score: 7

Influence is spreading the passion for your
work with contagious inspiration.

Think twice before you speak, because your words and influence will plant the seed of either success of failure in the mind of another.
Napoleon Hill

1 CHOOSE

We are human beings and human's being. We are not just humans having. What is the good of having things for the sake of it? We may feel like we own stuff. But, eventually it becomes evident that it can own us. Humans are social creatures and if we spend too much time on consumerism and buying the latest toy or gadget, then it may cause you more heartache than you expect. That new phone you upgraded to that cost you more than what is reasonable, in 3 months time will you be glad you bought it? Would it have enriched your life?

Take the latest iPhone release for example. Is it better than what you have now? Does it make phone calls, send texts and you can easily browse the internet and take pretty good photos?

The point is that it's important to be discerning with how a social society creates wants when there isn't one initially. We are consciously and subconsciously being subjected to marketing messages through our senses and dopamine hits to our brain on a daily basis. It's relentless. Instead of being negatively influenced by your social environment. Let's start to be the influencers and socialise influence. It's empowering and certainly builds confidence. Not only in being able to put up psychological defences to being manipulated or influenced with negative intention. But, also to gain the ability to influence others for good.

- Important because you'll become aware of what is the current reality is when it comes to psychological and social manipulation by the media and other people. Awareness is a great start.

- Important because you'll know how to defend yourself for negative influence in your life. You'll be poised to block toxic people and media messages from harming you. This includes dopamine hits and addictive feedback loops on social media, such as Facebook and Twitter.

Did you know that approximately 350 million people around the world are believed to meet the clinical definition of an addiction because of their Facebook habits?

I used to be addicted to Facebook. To be honest I still am to a certain extent. Now I set boundaries for myself.

- Use the IF-WHEN-THEN method. For example, IF you see an advert pops up on your favourite social media feed for Junk food such as chocolate or unhealthy burgers, WHEN you're mindlessly scrolling your social media feed. THEN go make a drink. This will reset the never-ending dopamine hit feedback loop that is, in fact, designed into the system to make you do just that. Scroll and scroll and more scrolling. The longer you spend on social media, the more advertising revenue the social media platform makes. This is good for investors and corporate profits. But, it is certainly not good for your brain, physical and mental health.

- Use an internet blocker or app on your phone or laptop that shuts down access to the internet after a certain amount of time. This will put influence and control back in your hands instead of online distractions and negative influences. How much time do you think you've wasted scrolling online? Be honest with yourself.

It may sound somewhat macabre and dark but imagine you've come to the end of your life and all that you can remember is what you saw online whilst scrolling social media. Your time is precious. Make sure you're mindful of how you're being influenced to spend it online. It's time to take the power back. Take your power back.

So, why the mindless social media scrolling?

Have you ever got to the point where you don't know why you've spent the last hour on social media?

Let's stop the scroll shall we!?

What are the benefits of socialising influence, of becoming influential?

Number one:

- Practising being sociable and knowledgeable is a tool to learn that builds confidence. So when you decide to make a choice to become influential your sphere of influence increases.

- Your thirst for knowledge deepens because you're motivated to learn more, to be more. It's a powerful cycle of learning, growth, progress and influence.

As you seek out more knowledge in various forms. It could be from reading, could be from enquiry, could be from research, or from searching and researching the Internet. It could be from using valid, credible sources, resources, people, and learning institutions such as universities or libraries.

Learn something.

Ask a question and get an answer. Create another question, which in turn creates another, which increases your knowledge each time.

Number two:

- You start off with the foundations of knowledge, the fundamentals, the basics. If you want to learn something of interest. Start with the basic foundational knowledge then you can start to delve into the greater details of that knowledge, which should be the branches and the leaves. And then your knowledge and understanding begins to take root and becomes implanted in your mind and then your understanding, therefore creating greater understanding of that knowledge.

- Going deeper with understanding. Elon Musk uses the analogy of a tree for knowledge and learning. With respect to social influence, learning new knowledge and being able to apply it takes greater understanding, so if you'd start off with the foundations. For example, a tree has to be solid. The stump. The foundation that has its roots. And branches and leaves and so on. A greater understanding of the knowledge is learnt. It is great to have a basic knowledge. Even better to understand that knowledge on a deeper level so that you can apply it. It takes theory to practise idea to action.

Once you can take action and share your knowledge freely with others, you can then get into esoteric knowledge, which is more specialised knowledge that you can use for specific types of problems and challenges. It depends on how far you want to go down the rabbit hole.

Number three:

This is really important, and socialising influence with respect to psychology and confidence builds stronger social connections. Then social and society in cultures. Are humans different in various parts of the world?

Online and digital or offline and analogue? A great sense of community can be built by growing your network. Human beings can benefit by building stronger social connections. By making you feel happier, and more connected. You've got a support network; you can be influenced by other people, and you can also influence other people. It's a double-edged sword. It works both ways. It can be a great thing to build a social network of people. Diverse areas of expertise and knowledge, life stages, socio-economic status. Individuals that are different from you. The more diverse your network is, the more far-reaching and stronger your social connections will be. Therefore the more influence you will have.

In addition, the concept of the dialectic is important as well, because when you have a conversation you'll have the opportunity to interact with different people. Various knowledge and skill sets will have an effect on outcomes. Beautiful relationships will be developed and ideas will blossom into action. Both parties can bring something new to the conversation, and you will both learn from it and move forward and progress.

How do we do that? How do we increase knowledge? How do we gain higher knowledge to improve the standard, and how do we build super-strong social connections to socialise influence?

It can be difficult for some people—myself included initially, but not any more— to ask for help. As blokes, we have been conditioned
by society to think that asking for help is a sign of weakness. I am saying that it definitely is not. It is a sign of courage and strength. The more you ask for help, the greater the benefit. Asking for help shows vulnerability, which is a sign of strength.
To put yourself out there, you are being courageous and brave, and it shows strength. People will

genuinely want to help you. People will want to get to know you by you simply asking for help.

Psychologically, people really appreciate when you ask them for help, because it shows you respect them. Humans genuinely want to help others if asked. If they do decide to help you, in their mind, they will tend to think and feel they like you because they've made a decision to help you. Even if they've never met you before. It's a great way of initiating a social connection.

It's a good idea to pick people who you think have the skills, aptitude or the knowledge to help you. It'll be more beneficial for everyone.

A psychological concept of social proof is when a person sees a group of other humans doing something. It is the human tendency where one person is influenced by another, by seeing elements of proof of a certain behaviour. For example, I walked nonchalantly into a local Brisbane coffee shop. It was a typical Australian cafe with the air-conditioning blasting out cool air and the sweet scent of coffee beans being ground by the skilled barista.

What do I see?

I witness about 80 per cent of the people, either in couples or sat in groups of friends, they were looking down at their mobile phone. Not really engaged in conversation. I almost went to grab my phone from my pocket and start looking at it, and I asked myself and thought, *Hang on a moment!* I was totally being influenced by social proof. What I mean by that is if other people are doing things in groups then others are likely to be influenced socially to do the same. Including myself. I'm only human after all.

Social proof is powerful, so be mindful of it. You can use it positively.

The more great things you do—for example, asking for help, helping others, being charitable— that creates positive social proof for more people. I hope you grasp this and go with it. I'm sure you will. For example, there's a group of people jogging together and having fun and exercising. That's a great form of social proof because I might keep running because other people are doing it. It's a form of positive social influence with health benefits. Physically and mentally.

Did you know that confidence is the degree to which you believe your actions will result in a positive outcome? So influence yourself by being influenced positively by others by asking for help. But beware of the influencing power of social proof.

Once you practice being more self-aware you will become more confident because you'll be more certain that your actions will result in a positive outcome.

Another solution for socialising influence with respect to confidence psychology is reciprocity. If you do something for someone, it's highly likely they will do something for you. For example, if you give someone a lift to somewhere in your car, they're highly likely to help you, in future, to do the same, give you a lift, or can help you with something else, because this type of positive influence is the influencing power of reciprocity. It's the same as if someone gives you a gift, you feel the need to give them a gift in return. So share your gift and socialise influence in your own unique way.

We all have unique DNA, and by being aware of socialising influence and practising being socially influential, you will definitely become more confident. Remember, confidence is on a spectrum that can change day to day, even hour to hour. You can increase your confidence, you can sustain it, and you can also lose it. So it's great to practise it daily.

So here is your challenge should you choose to accept it:

- Walk into a coffee shop and walk up to a perfect stranger and ask for help. Ask them any questions. For example, do you know where the bathroom is please?

Go on!

What's the worst that could happen?

Purely by doing this challenge you will build confidence because you will have overcome a fear. You will have stepped out of your comfort zone. This is where growth happens and it's absolutely life-changing. I can assure you.

Please feel free to let me know how it goes.

2 AWARENESS

Socialising influence is important because it creates massive confidence. You'll be practising building a strong foundation of influence in a social environment. Humans are social creatures and so need to be social to create influence and improve self-confidence. It's important to be mindful of seeing life as a work in progress.

The benefits of socialising influence with respect to awareness is remembering that you have the ability, as a human being to have influence over yourself.

Number one. It is empowering.
Number two. It's influential.
Number three. It's persuasive.
Empowering. Influential and persuasive.

It's empowering because it gives you a great sense of personal and individual power, and you have the ability and wherewithal to be powerful in your own right, with influence. Using influencing skills, use your own influence to create change within yourself, change in your behaviour, and then eventually influence others positively.

Persuasion. By persuading others it's selling an idea by using various methods. For example, in an interview, you are selling yourself in order to persuade the employer that you will be a great employee. It's all about creating emotion, focusing on a motion. Emotion creates motion, movement, always moving forward with your energy.

So there are three solutions to focus on with regard to awareness and socialising influence.

Number one is by utilising the halo effect. What the halo effect is, is what you do first and what you focus on. And what people assume or know about you the first time they hear about you or you're spoken of when they meet you has an effect on future understandings of you and how influential you can be. For example, Brad Pitt. He is known, if you meet him for the first time, as a famous actor, and he has won awards for acting. Therefore, the halo effect is, if you know that he's a good award-winning actor, then he must be great in other areas such as public speaking, learning words, learning lines, being sociable, being kind.

The halo effect is very powerful.

Number two. Body language. Use your body to talk. Be open to others. More importantly, listen. Be mindful and aware of other people's body language. Listen with all your senses.

Did you know that 80 percent of communication is non-verbal? Think about that.

Understanding body language is an important part of socialising influence. An example of that is if you're in a group of people and one person that you're focused on is pointing their feet at you, in your direction. It means they're interested in you and what you have to say. If their feet are pointing away from you, the opposite is the case. It's nuances like this that are important to be aware of, because that can help for you to be social, with respect to building influence. You can also focus on people's arms. If their arms are crossed, it means they are defensive about what you have to say, and it will be difficult to influence them and persuade them. If their arms are crossed be open with yours. By opening your body language and showing the palms of your hands and with open arms it'll be a lot easier to influence and persuade this particular person. Or if it's cold outside, they could just be cold and want to warm their body by crossing their arms. More often than not, it is because they are being defensive.

Also, if you're in a group of people and something funny happens or someone makes a joke and everyone laughs, the person who looks at you while laughing is generally the person that feels most connected to you. It is something to be mindful of.

Number three. Heart focus. What I mean by that is, by having a focus on a heart connection instead of purely thinking logically, which is a great thing in its own right, being more connected to your emotions with respect to other people and other human beings is great. It connects us all. It connects you to the next person. We all have hearts. We all have emotions. Instead of boiling situations down to your logic, it's a great idea to practise being empathetic and heart-focused and emotionally connected to an understanding of other people, because that will improve your socialised influence.

Did you know that a healthy heart beats an average of 100,000 times a day and over a human lifetime creates enough energy to drive a truck to the moon and back?

Be mindful of others with respect to your emotions, their emotions. Your heart and their heart.

3 NOW

To socialise influence and to become influential is a great thing to practise and learn in everyday life, because the benefits are exponential.
There are three main parts to socialising influence. All three are as important as the other.

The benefits are threefold.

Number one, becoming influential builds confidence.

Number two, it builds more confidence.

Number three, it builds even more confidence.

So this is massively important—being influential, practising influence, and socialising influence. There is potential for massive confidence. How do we do that and what are the solutions?

Firstly, influence yourself first. Socialise with yourself. Start to enjoy your own company. Set time aside to be with yourself. By influencing yourself first, you're influencing the most important person in your life—you. By building yourself up, by liking yourself, by spending quality time with yourself, you start to be able to be confident spending time on your own, confident in your own presence, and confident with how influential you are with yourself, to yourself. For example, persuade yourself, empower yourself and influence yourself to do certain practices every single day. Once you commit to practising influencing yourself every single day, it becomes a habit, like brushing your teeth.

For example, you can say to yourself today 'I will not buy a coffee. I will save the $5 that I was going to spend on buying a coffee, and I will put that into my savings.' Once you do that, once you commit to that, you've influenced yourself to change your behaviour for a future outcome. You can intellectualise it. You can think about it logically. However, the most important part of influencing yourself is making it emotional and deep to your core, to your core values, whatever it is, whether it's not buying a coffee, whether it's using $5 to invest to start with, or whether it's having a cold shower.

For example, I influence myself every single day by starting off with a nice warm shower, and then I turn the warm water to cold water, blasting over my body every single morning for twenty seconds. I have to influence myself to turn the warm tap off and take the hit of cold water. The benefits are amazing. It immediately wakes me up in the early morning, it's invigorating and great for the skin. The most important thing is that I've influenced myself to get out of my comfort zone and do that every single day.

Will you do it? I must admit it feels a bit weird to start with and it's certainly not easy to turn the hot tap off.

Go on.

You can do it!

There is another solution for socialising your influences. An almost perfect gem of simple life advice is to meditate every single day. Talking about the shower, you could do it for five seconds in the shower. Simply relax your mind for five seconds while warm water going over your head.

Breathe in.

Breathe out.

Repeat, focusing on just your breath. Start with five seconds. The next day, go to ten. The next day, twenty. Then eventually build it to five minutes, and then go from there.

The benefits of meditation are amazing. You start to become more influential, you start to become more confident, you'll be happier, you'll have more energy, and you have created
a powerful habit, practice and behaviour that will help you be confident.

Another solution is to use the phrase 'If you can't, you must'.

I repeat that. 'If you can't, you must.'

For example, 'I can't do that, because I haven't got enough time.' If you can't, you must. You must make time. You must create time. If it's important to you, you will make time to do it. Everyone has twenty-four hours in a day.

Create your priorities.

If you can't, you must. So next time you find yourself saying 'I can't do it', reframe and tell yourself, 'If I can't, I must.'

12

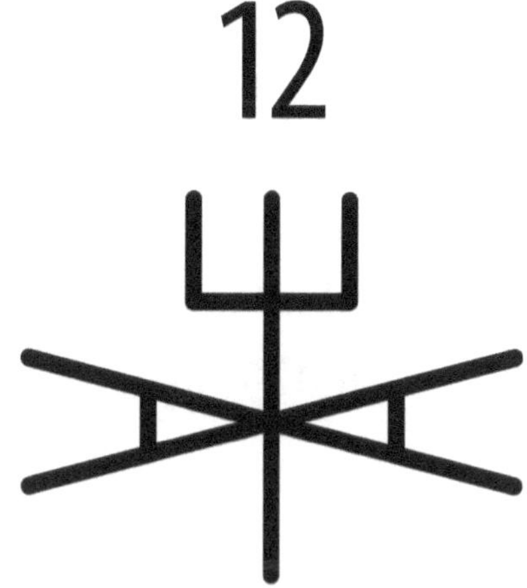

THINK STRATEGICALLY

Power-Up Score: 6

The biggest risk is not taking any risk,
the only strategy that is guaranteed
to fail is not taking risks.
Zuckerberg

There's only one growth strategy: work hard
William Hague

The essence of strategy is choosing what not to do.
Michael Porter

Strategy is nothing without
effective leaders to execute.
Global Leadership Forecast 2018, EY,
Building a Better Working World

Who you become as you reach your goals is
more important than reaching the goals.
Jim Rohn

1 CHOOSE

Strategy builds confidence, because you have a solid framework and action plan of what to do and, more importantly, what *not* to do. With clarity comes power, and with power is strength. You'll gain mental strength, because you'll know exactly what you're focused on and why. It's like a pilot plotting a course to their destination. Careful and strategic planning is considered before take-off. Safety, weather, weight, fuel, and other variables come into play. For example, a pilot is skilled in the technical aspects of flying a plane. She is also skilled in map-reading, leadership, and collaborating with her team, especially the air traffic controllers. Once the plane is airborne after a successful take-off, the captain must now manage and control the plane to get all passengers to the agreed destination safely and in good time.

All of a sudden, there's a faint shudder, and the aircraft tilts violently, with no warning.

What happened?

Now to ensure the safety of all four hundred passengers, the captain must adapt to a potentially life-threatening situation with calmness, speed, and clarity.

Strategic thinking is all about using the power of your mind to execute your strategy. 'What is my strategy?' you ask. Patience, my friend. We'll get to that. But first, let's go back to our captain, piloting the 300,000 kg flying chunk of metal hurtling through the sky at 900 km/h.

What is going through our pilot's mind? Panic? No. If this captain panics and loses control of her thoughts, four hundred humans' lives are at risk of being lost too.

So now is the time to see if the strategy works in reality. All the years of training, flight school, leadership skills, growth mindset, and technical mastery comes into play. This is it.

In a calm and controlled manner, our captain makes a critical assessment of the situation in the most effective way she knows. I leave the technical details to your imagination. Then our composed pilot delivers a clear message to the passengers: 'Hello, ladies and gentlemen, boys and girls. What you just experienced was a result of a small foreign body entering one of our engines. I'm here to reassure you that everything is going to be okay and it's under control. You may feel some unfamiliar movements of the plane. Please do your best to remain calm. Our highly trained flight attendants are here for you, as am I. Thank you for choosing to fly with . . .' You get the story.

Now the story ends successfully, with our courageous pilot flying the plane to the nearest landing strip by following emergency protocol. You see, it's all part of the strategy.

Turns out a griffon vulture had flown directly into one of the jet engines! It was a serious emergency situation. With leadership, critical thinking, calmness of mind, training, and execution of a strategy, our captain literally saved four hundred lives from death.

The importance of strategic thinking cannot be underestimated.

How will you incorporate strategic thinking into your daily life?

2 AWARENESS

Thinking strategically is massively important because it helps you open your mind in thinking of a way that is more likely for you to reach your goals connected to your core values. So in a sense, it's a way of thinking by zooming out and observing the observer. You are the observer. You're thinking about your environment, in your environment. However, when you begin to think strategically and practise strategic thinking, you begin to observe the observer. You can look and think from a different perspective, which in turn will help you realise that thinking strategically is beneficial not only for yourself but also other people. So it's a practice. The more you practise, the better you will become.

The first aspect of strategic thinking involves your goals, what you will do?

SMART goals.

S is for *specific.*
M is for *measurable.*
A is for *attainable.*
R is for relevant.
T is for *time-sensitive.*

Smart goals enable you to be specific about your goals. It's highly likely you'll be able to achieve them, because you have clarified exactly what your goals are, and clarity is power.

Now write down your goals on a piece of paper. Writing on a piece of paper ensures 80 percent of retention, so your goal starts to act yourself into your mind and your psyche. Once you've done this, you can create your strict action plan by thinking strategically.

So start to purposefully write the following letters on a clean sheet of paper or simply type them up on you smartphone or laptop.

S

M

A

R

T

Why do you want to achieve this one smart goal?

Why is it important to you?

Then write it down.

For me, the most important purpose for my goal is, one of my goals is to spend quality time with my son, Zachary. That's my purpose. My purpose is to spend quality time with my son, because my values are family, love, and spending time with my son.

Time is more valuable than money and two children. Love equals time, time spent with them.

Then you write your results. What results do you want? Be specific. For example, I would like to spend two hours every other day with my son outside in nature. Be as specific as possible, and then you can write one to three results—specific results—you want to achieve. Then you write your purposeful action plan. So what specific actions are you going to take with respect to purpose and results you want to achieve? What actions are you going to take? For example, schedule time in your calendar at 4 p.m. I'm going to spend time between 4pm and 6pm. I'm going to pick my son, Zachary, up from the daycare. I'm going to go and play football with him in the park for two hours.

That's the action plan.

You can create one to three actions that you're going to take, then from those actions, you can break them down into priorities. You can prioritise the action, to most important meeting and least important, and then you can categorise them into two times. Then you can schedule them. What gets scheduled gets done.

As a conclusion, thinking strategically is massively important to reaching your goals. Use your SMART goals to realise your strategy. Execute your strategy to get to your goals, whether they are short-term or long-term, and they're really purposeful and important to you. By thinking strategically, it increases your motivation—relentless motivation— and increases your energy. And energy is awesome.

Three challenges:

1. Write down one smart goal.
2. Write down your results, a result you want. And your 'why' your purpose? And one massive action plan to get to that result.
3. Schedule one of those action plans into your Google Calendar or a calendar that you use.

3 NOW

When you think strategically, it's massively powerful in how you create your reality, your personal reality, and your personality. It improves focus, because you're focused on where you want to go, what you want to do with your life. Your daily life for your entire life. This includes, business, relationships, and financially.

Clarity is power. So what is strategy, and what is thinking strategically?

It's opening your mind to a way of thinking about how you'll get to where you want to go. What you will do and what you won't do determines your long-term strategy. It's a dynamic action plan focused on a long-term future outcome or result.

Ask yourself these questions:

What's most important to you?

What are your core values?

Where do you want to be in five years' time or even ten years' time or beyond?

Building a foundational structure helps you plan out your strategy, what you will and won't do. Here's an analogy. An aircraft and pilot leave the airport. They know the coordinates. They know where they need to get to, and know their destination. Beforehand, they have a strategy and a goal. There are various situations and variables. For example, the weather. The weather could change. For example, slight adjustments need to be made during the process, so the pilot might have to adjust the route slightly. However, he'll still get to the destination, being adaptable and making slight adjustments, focusing on the process to enable the outcome to happen which is the destination.

Benjamin Franklin said 'Failing to plan is planning to fail', so make sure you have a great plan in place by thinking strategically about what you can do.

Once you've answered your questions honestly and authentically, you can reverse-engineer
an action plan, your dynamic action plan, your strategy. Work backwards, say, in five years' time, four years, three years, two years, one year, up until today. Then you'll have a great framework to execute your plan.

Start to meditate. Meditating regularly gives your mind and body a gap of time and space, some space and time to connect with who you are, your mind, and your body, and it really helps you zoom out of all the noise, of all the chatter that's going on in the world, in your world, and all the distractions. This helps you refocus and gain balance in mind. It helps creative thinking and being able to execute your strategy.

In conclusion, thinking strategically is massively important in realising your life goals by implementing a dynamic action plan with what you will do and what you won't do, connected to your values and goals. Have fun with it and be patient and enjoy the process.

Three challenges for you:

1. Meditate for two minutes in silence, focusing purely on your breath, simply inhaling and exhaling. If thoughts come to you, racing thoughts, observe them and let them be. Imagine your thoughts are wispy clouds that are moving across the sky with a gentle breeze.

2. Think of a creative idea. Think of a random object. Do your best to connect two seemingly random ideas together. To create a new idea, write down on a piece of paper two random items that come to mind. For example, it could be a banana and a cloud. Then think of an idea from those two items.

3. Think of your last argument with someone. It could have been a colleague, or it could have been a family member or partner. Think about how it made you feel, and then think in hindsight about how you could have implemented a strategy. How you could've thought strategically to create a better outcome for both parties to create a win–win outcome. Write it down. It's one for your archives.

13

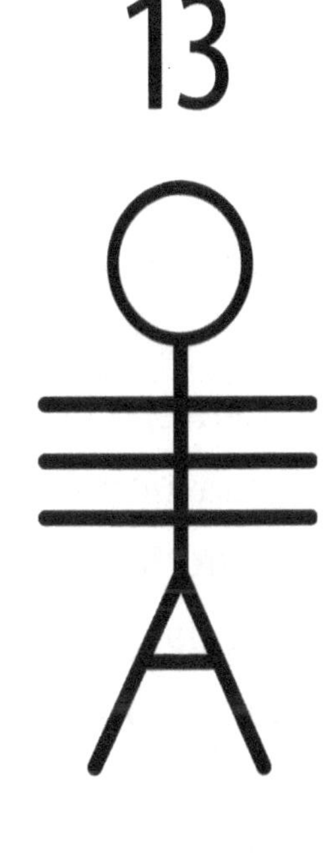

BE EXPONENTIAL

Power-Up Score: 9

In the age of exponential change we
need the power of diverse thinking.
Cathy Engelbert

Definition of *exponential growth*: when the rate of change is proportional to the current value of the function (human) = time, its value is exponential.

The obstacle is the pathway.

1 CHOOSE

'Be exponential.' What does that even mean? An exponential is a function of mathematics in its original meaning. You may have heard the term *exponential growth*, which refers to the rate of change, and value, mathematically speaking, is proportional to the function's current value. It is expressed by this formula: $y = ab^x$. If this makes no sense—and I completely understand if it doesn't—all will be clear in a moment. You see, words—or in this case, mathematical formulas—have their limitations. However, your imagination is unlimited.

'Be exponential' means be exponential with your thinking by starting to think exponentially, as in *you* become *the* function. By changing and growing exponentially, you will create and experience massive exponential growth in your lifetime. How freaking exciting is that? I'm excited for you! If you're not quite feeling it yet, please be patient, because it's worth it.

Once you become exponential by being exponential, your life will change dramatically, for the better. Guaranteed.

- Important because: you deserve to release your unlimited human potential. You are worthy. We all are. Just watch what happens. This is so exciting!

- Important because: you have one life only. Would you rather live a life of unrealised potential or an awesome life of released potential? The energy you'll experience once you practise this way of thinking and being will be unstoppable. Be exponential. I challenge you. Let's do this, shall we?

Did you know that once you decide on a course of action, the simple act of the decision literally changes your life in that moment? It's as simple as asking yourself the question. 'Will I be exponential today?' Yes or no. You decide. By simply answering your own question, you take ownership of your life. You are now leading yourself. You are a leader and powerfully own your decisions. It's liberating. Do it!

Okay, so did you reply yes or no?

I used to overcomplicate things. If I had a dilemma or a choice, I would totally overthink it. Should I pick strawberry or chocolate ice cream for dessert? My past thought process: 'Hmm, if I choose chocolate, it will taste great because I know I like chocolate. I've tasted it before, and it's so damn good. Hey, but what if it's not the same ingredients and the taste is different from last time? Maybe I'll choose strawberry instead. I like strawberries, but I don't like it as much as chocolate. Damn, I can't decide.' This type of thinking leads to analysis paralysis, where you analyse a situation and don't come to a decision quickly. You're paralysed by overthinking. What I learnt is, listen to your heart, as opposed to listening too much to your head. What I mean by that is, do you love chocolate, or do you love strawberries? It makes it a hell of a lot easier to decide once you tap into this type of decision-making. Now I know deep down I love chocolate and really, really like strawberry. Now my decision is easy. I choose chocolate.

What would you decide? What's your chocolate-or-strawberry decision, and will you decide quicker with more heart than head in the future?

- Take the important step to simplify your decision-making to a yes-or-no answer. For example, will you be exponential? Yes or no?

- If in doubt, always make a decision. Even if you decide to wait or sleep on a decision, that's cool. What's most important is to take ownership of your power to decide. 'It is in your moments of decision that your destiny is shaped' (Tony Robbins).

Make decisions based on what your heart truly wants. You'll know when you truly know. Please be mindful of how your mind will try to interfere. Your brain is an awesome organic computer capable of immense intelligence and calculations, although it is simply a tool you can use to your advantage. Avoid analysis paralysis by tapping into a deeper level of thinking and feeling. This will improve with practice. How? By observing the observer. You are both the observer and the observed. This is being exponential.

2 AWARENESS

Thinking exponentially and practising being exponential everyday will change your perspective; therefore, your life will never be the same again.

- Important because: the way you think day in and day out determines the trajectory of your life. Do you want to live life on autopilot, or do you want to live an exponential life?

- Important because: psychology affects 80 percent of everything in your life. If you don't become aware of how you think, your glorious potential may never be released. That would not be cool. You have one life. Think wisely and choose how you think. Yes, you are in control—more than you know.

Did you know short-term memory lasts about fifteen to thirty seconds? (Peterson and Peterson, 1959).

As an energetic child, I was a daydreamer. I would imagine random scenarios in my mind's eye. What would it be like to fly to the sun on a beam of light? How would it feel to bend time and space? I was a freethinker. Fast-forward a few years into my teenage years. I became part of the MTV generation by watching music videos on a loop. I became brainwashed. My mind lost its imagination because it was fed a poor diet of flashing lights, music, and dopamine through this square electronic box in my family living room. At this stage, I was a linear thinker, limited in my scope of cognitive abilities. This is because your brain adapts with neuroplasticity, meaning it is shaped by input. Like a car engine, if you feed it poor-grade fuel, it will perform as you expect—poorly. Give your engine high-grade petrol and oil, and the result will be high performance. Your brain is similar. Now after years of reading, critical thinking, a degree in psychology, and daily personal development and growth from nutritious, beautiful knowledge and awareness, I am an exponential thinker. Why do you think I'm writing this book right now?

- Write ideas down within thirty seconds of having the thought, or you may forget your brilliant idea!

- Imagine you're on a spaceship that can travel at the speed of light. Open your mind and view any situation from the perspective of the sun. Zoom out from your position and view from afar.

- Imagine 300 years from now. How will this situation affect you in 300 years? By doing so, you will expand your thinking and, with practice, become an exponential thinker.

3 NOW

By expanding your mind outside the limitation of linear thinking (1, 2, 3) to the unlimited realm of the exponential (1, 2, 4, 8, 16, 32, and so on), you will come alive. Your brain will be firing at a higher level of awareness and imagination. See what happens. It's magnificent. You will create a future to be excited for every single morning.

14

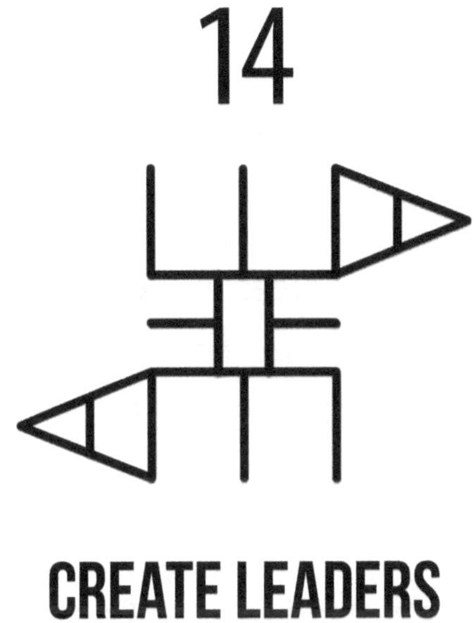

CREATE LEADERS

Great leaders create great leaders

1 CHOOSE

2 AWARENESS

3 NOW

Great leaders create great leaders

Will you accept this ultimate challenge?

What's the worst that can happen? Seriously?

You must.

It's your duty.

Well, to be fair it's your choice. Choose wisely my friend.

Creating leaders is the most important purpose of leadership.

- Important because: leadership is more than you. It's more than the ego. You create 'we'. 'We' creates 'us'. By creating more leaders, you become a great leader.

- Important because: creating leaders is cyclical. The leaders you help create, in turn, become great leaders, and so on. These new leaders, in turn, creating more great leaders. It's exponential. Be exponential.

Did you know that 'contrary to the opinion of many people, leaders are not born'? 'Leaders are made, and they are made by effort and hard work' (Vince Lombardi).

Once I made a firm decision to be a leader, I learnt, mainly through reading and learning by listening to others, that the most important purpose of being a leader and practising leadership is to create more leaders. By leading by example, you set the precedence for the next generation of leaders. That fateful day, on a beautiful spring morning in Brisbane, Australia, 2017, I committed to being a leader and to focusing on creating more leaders. I did not make this promise to anyone else, not my father, my mother, my sister, or my brother. I made this decision to me, myself, and I.

I said, 'I am Adam Bowcutt, and I am a leader.' That day, my life changed—

forever.

- Say three times in the mirror 'I am [your name], and I am a leader'.

- Go on. I'll wait. I'm not going to sugar-coat it. Doing this is extremely difficult for some people because it means getting out of your comfort zone. You may feel silly or weird. You may feel embarrassed. None of this matters, because the result is more important than the method. You will literally see yourself saying to yourself that you're a leader. It's a powerful thing. Okay, did you do it? If you did, congratulations! If you didn't, that's fine too.

I'm not here to judge. However, think about why you didn't do it.

- Reach out to three people in your immediate network. They could be family members, friends, colleagues—anyone you know. Now say something completely honest that you see in them, like a positive strength. Pick one thing and simply share it with them. You can call them by phone, text them, or use social media messaging. The important thing is to share your message with them authentically. For example, I love sending messages to friends that simply say 'You are awesome'. Imagine receiving a message like that from someone you know and believing it because you know deep down that the message is true.

By creating leaders, you enter the next level of leadership. Call it what you will—excellence, greatness, or radness. You end up making a positive impact on this world. How awesome is that?

PS. You are awesome.

15

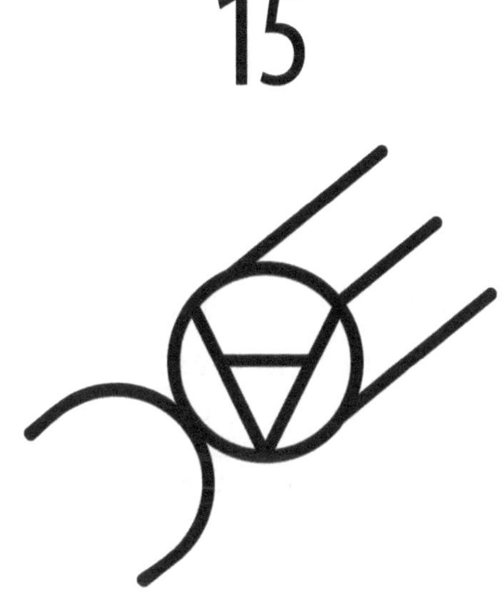

YOUR LEGACY

Power-Up Score: 9

'You are going to die.'—Physics

1 CHOOSE

2 AWARENESS

3 NOW

You are going to die.

Let me say that again. You are going to die.

Have a think about that. Take a deep breath. Go on. Now imagine you're on your deathbed. You are literally going to die. What is going through your mind? Have you lived your best life and realised your unlimited potential? You have? Yes! That's awesome! Perfect, so now that you've imagined this, let's do something about it, shall we? You must have absolutely no regrets, because those things you wish you did (snap yourself back to your imaginary deathbed for just a moment), they are you. They are your potential.

What's the worst that can happen if you don't do the exact things you want to do in your life? You die.

What happens if you don't do the exact things you want to do in your life? You die.

We are all going to die. It's simply a fact of life. Now, what will you choose to do while you are still alive?

Now you have the ultimate power to decide what your legacy will be. So, my friend, what will it be?

- Important because: a legacy is bigger than you. After your body has perished and you are no more, what you leave on this amazing planet Earth is your legacy, nobody else's. It is uniquely yours because you created it. The fact that your legacy will no longer literally serve you means it is bigger than you, bigger than your ego, larger than life itself. Your life is massively important. There's no denying that. But what's equally important is creating your legacy today. Now.

- Important because: a legacy helps you live forever. Sounds a bit far-fetched, doesn't it? A bit out there, slightly woo-woo. Okay, perhaps your physical body won't live forever. Our body is fallible. It is a beautiful machine that we live inside and use to do stuff, really cool stuff—live. But it's finite. Your body will decay. It will fade. On the other hand, your legacy is infinite. Your essence, your source of power, energy, and confidence. You will live forever through your legacy. Most importantly, with a focus on creating your legacy, you will live with massive confidence, self-belief, passion, and purpose, because you'll be building your legacy today. Now once you begin this journey, it is amazing. You'll have more energy, clarity, super-strong mental health, and confidence as a result of a daily focus on creating your legacy.

Did you know that 56 million people die each year? That's 6,316 people taking their last breath each hour.

How does that make you feel?

I used to think only about myself. I was very ego-focused. How will I do this? How will I do that? How will this affect me? What do I get? Notice how many *I*s there are. Once you choose to shift your focus to creating a legacy, you begin to reduce the *I*s and increase the *we*s.

The benefit of doing this is gargantuan. No man is an island. Let's rephrase that, shall we? No human is an island. We are social creatures. We need one another not only to survive but to thrive.

- Write down your eulogy on a piece of paper. Go grab a paper and pen right now. Okay, cool. Now imagine you've just died. It's not the most delightful of thoughts, but it's important, because it will help you refocus your attention. All right, so back to your thoughts. So you've died, and you're watching your funeral unfold. What will loved ones, family, friends, and colleagues hear from this eulogy, these words describing your life? What kind of life did you live? What kind of person were you? What will you be remembered for? Once you've thought deeply about these things, simply write them down on a piece of paper. Now this is reality. Those words are real. The work now is to reverse-engineer how you will create this life you want to be remembered for. Are you ready?

- Give to charity. Pick a charity that's close to your values. What is important to you? Were you once extremely poor? Give to a charity that helps the homeless. Did your mother suffer from depression? Give to a mental health charity. You've already given to the Lifeline Mental Health suicide prevention charity by buying this book. Thank you! Once you commit to giving a portion of your wealth to charity, you commit to helping others. Helping others is one of the best habits you can nurture with respect to your legacy. It will help others less fortunate than you, of course. However, more importantly, you'll become a person of great value because you are being of service to others. It's a positive self-fulfilling prophecy, because the more people you give to and help, the more you'll become a better person of value. In turn, you'll help even more people, and so the cycle continues and grows. It's awesome. Start giving! Charity doesn't always mean financial giving. It can also be giving your valuable time by volunteering or simply helping with pro-bono work with a skill you have that others need.

A legacy is a powerful focus, and it nurtures kindness and energy that serves you and others.

***

Zachary - Aged 4:

"Daddy, what made the world?

Daddy - Aged 40:

"Energy"

Zachary: "How did energy make the world?"

Daddy: "Great question Zac. I highly recommend you asking a variety of people this question because you'll get a better, balanced answer"

Zachary: "..."

***

Energy

Pssst...

I'll let you into a little secret. This isn't the end, yet.

There is a super-secret final chapter somewhere out there in the ether. But where is it and how do you access it?

Your challenge:

Within the pages of this book there are two codes hidden in plain sight.

Once you locate the two codes you must add the two codes together to reveal the answer.

This answer is the third code.

This number will lead you to a site that will give you access to the super-secret chapter of insane dumbfounding knowledge

Will you take the following 3 steps? :

Step 1

Go to the chapter in this book that has a power-up score of 7 and the title quote is 'You can't understand someone until you've walked a mile in their shoes'. Make a mental note of the chapter number.

Step 2

Go to the chapter in this book that has a power-up score of 6 and the title quote is 'Words have energy and power with the ability to help, to heal, to hinder, to hurt, to harm, to humiliate, and to humble' Make a mental note of the chapter number.

Step 3

Add together the two numbers you remember from step 1 and 2. What is the answer? Now go to this chapter number and do it confidently.

(Hint: It's at the centre of a circle)

Do it, now.

Confidently. Go to www.adambowcutt.com.au and press LEARN MORE and then enter the code number to the box that says "What's your question?* Then press SEND. You will then be sent the super-secret chapter...

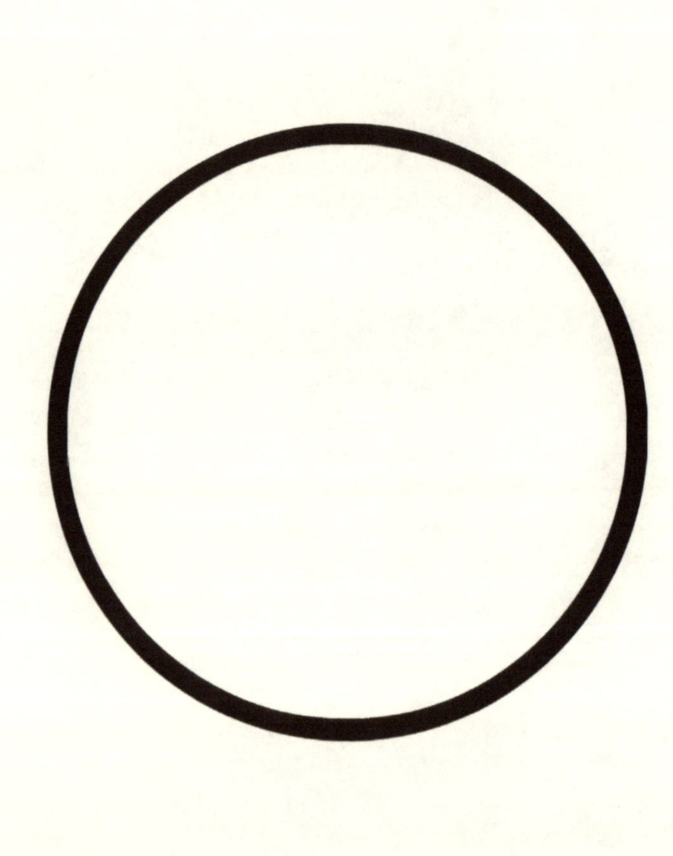

INDEX

9 781796 005738